I0044825

Portrait of a Non-Traditional Politician

Portrait of a Non-Traditional Politician

By Brian Taylor

ISBN: 978-0-578-01525-5

Foreword

The 7th Congressional District of Virginia has made some very dramatic changes demographically speaking of course. With census being taken every 10 years, current demographics is outdated to say the least. The district was created March 4, 1789 and had dual representation during the Civil War until March 18, 1865. Representation was inactive during the Restoration of the Union period.

On January 26, 1870 a Union Conservative Lewis McKenzie was seated as the first Representative. He was defeated by, (the first Democrat to hold this position) Elliot M. Braxton. 11 Democrats represented this district, compared to seven Republicans. It was a Democrat that represented this district the longest. Rep. Burr P. Harrison served from November 5, 1946 until he retired on January 3, 1963. Rep. Harrison successor was another Democrat John O. Marsh who also served until he retired eight years later.

Rep. J. Kenneth Robinson was the third Republican elected to represent the district. Rep. Robinson held the seat for 14 years, longer than any other Republican to date. The district has been consecutively represented by notable Republicans, including former Governor and former Senator George Allen and the current Representative Eric I. Cantor, whom is the Republican Whip.

In 1990 the district became a Republican Stronghold due to forced redistricting by the Justice Department. So how does a Blue Dog Democrat, like me take this district back? Well from watching the trends of the last few years, I have come up with a strong campaign strategy. Of course, I am not going to put the entire campaign strategy in this book. But, one thing I will say is that all opponents were not able to reach enough people. This book is just part of that strategy. GET THE MESSAGE OUT!

Portrait of a Non-Traditional Politician

Introduction

In 2008 CNN in conjunction with Essence Magazine did a special documentary on being Black in America. During the build up to airing of this two part, two day nationally televised show, I remember saying and thinking "finally, it is about time." I remember after seeing the shows I was a bit disappointed. To me it only eloquently restated the issues in Black America. The issues that was prevalent in a different era. The problem I had with the show is that it did not go in-depth as to how much black America has achieved. Not to say that a black American does not have any issues today, because black Americans do. If they would have gone more in-depth in all the issues it would have set the criteria for inevitable change.

The other problem I had with this show and one of the reasons for this book is that they made no mention of being Black in American Politics. No mention what so ever of our politics or our sudden rise to middle class. They some what mention a middle class family who moved to a majority white neighborhood. Black middle class neighborhoods do exist in America. What is odd is that before black Americans entered into the middle class there was only one middle class America. Now there exist a lower and upper. Thanks to or should I say No Thanks to the Bush Administration there now exist a very thin line between upper lower and the lower middle. Now if one is totally confused, one can now understand why there exist serious poverty problems in America. Just when one thinks I have finally reached a goal, someone moves the line.

The reason I decided to write this book is to introduce you to the new Non-Traditional Politicians. Who are these new politicians? Where can you find these politicians? How do you recognize these new politicians? Here too, most people have it wrong. They are not published in any law journal; they are not apart of any Bar Association; they are not a partner of any law firm; in fact, they are not lawyers. They are not corporate executives; they are not political interns; although they are politically intelligent, some of them do not hold academic degrees as of yet. They are the average Jane's; the average Joe's, living and maintaining life. They are apart of the new Middle Class of America. They are the politicians next door.

This book is written to inspire, motivate and activate the politician within you the reader. To help make it possible to recognize the politician next door to you the reader. For you the reader to support that politician next door to you. Contrary to popular belief, we can make a difference. It does not matter your party affiliation, just think outside the box. Let your own conscience and views be your guide.

Table of Contents

The Early Years

Portrait of a Patriot

I remember watching a child saluting a horse drawn carriage that contained his father's casket on television. I then stood up and saluted too, causing even more tears to flow from my parents and their friends eyes. I didn't know why I did it, maybe because we were the same age and I was copying his actions. I just knew it was something that had to be done. I did not know at that time that this action would be repeated three more times. As three more childhood heroes of mine were taken from us when assassinator's bullets hit their marks: Brother Minister Malcolm X; Rev. Dr. Martin L. King Jr., and Robert F. Kennedy.

Although young, I recall the outrage of adults during these times, I even recall my outrage when Rev. Dr. Martin L. King Jr. was killed, the anger turning to fear when the lights went out in New York during the riots. I remember me and my male cousins guarding the bedroom doors, (baseball bats in hands) where the females of the family, was instructed to stay. My uncle took his stance at the front door of the house, (rifle in hand) in the famous "Any Means Necessary" pose of Malcolm X. The next day while walking through the neighborhood to find the damage created the night before. I still to this day don't understand what was the rioting and looting for, what was to be accomplished by these acts of violence.

I was raised in a two parent household with three brothers and three sisters; this being the start up of the single parent household, this situation was unusal. My mother was the typical housewife, caring for us all. My father was a college graduate and quite the track star. He had set several records at City College that still are unbroken today. He worked two jobs to make sure that we had food to eat, clothes to wear and a roof over our heads. We never wanted for anything, thanks to him being an only child and his parents helping financially. Two of my three uncles were Vietnam Veterans, and my paternal grandfather was a veteran as well, which inspired me to become a soldier one day. I attended a local catholic school that put me on the road to becoming a professional basketball player, or so I thought. Being at work so much my father was never truly there to give moral support and guidance, not to say that I loved him any less or that he failed me as a father, love in our household was expressed through actions, not the spoken words.

I started school a year early, it was one of five Catholic Elementary School located in Harlem, New York. Instead of starting in kindergarten, I was placed in a first grade class with two older cousins. I remember for the very first week, going to school and crying to be paid by nuns to stop. The money collected was spent after school with other siblings in the local candy store. After that first week I buckled down and proceeded to work. I was promoted to the second grade just as my parents had gotten accepted for housing in a new city development. At that time the City Development was majority middle income residents, lower income was often found in private owned tenement Housing. These private owned housing often became abandoned, which caused the change in the City Developments, which forced the middle income residents to find either: Co-Op or Condo housing, or purchase their own home.

We moved in that summer which I had to change schools. My parents wanted me to grow and learn with children my age and made me repeat the first grade against the advice of the Principal and my pleas. I ended up ahead of the class, and became bored with school. I took on an interest in sports, two hand tag football, basketball, volleyball and bowling in particular.

As I watched the CNN special, it reinforced my belief that we have come a long way, but there exists an even a longer journey ahead. We the black people in America have to first realize and accept that racism does exist. It may be very covert at times…but it does exist. The other thing we must realize and accept that trouble will surely come…but it does not have to overcome. Black Americans need to stop considering ourselves the victims of racism. Black Americans can now control ones own destiny. I am not saying that all white people are racists just as I am not saying that all black people are intolerant of the white race. What I am saying about race is that there should only exist one that truly matters today, the Human Race.

As we stand on the threshold of American Political History, I have to agree with the first Black Man to become the President of the United States point. That point being; black people need to take more responsibility in their homes. Black men take back your place in the family structure. Black women allow that man his place in the family structure. Black people we need to display love and respect for the opposite sex so that our children will grow up with the same attitude. A woman can not raise a man just as a man can not raise a woman. It takes both a man and a woman to raise a child.

The CNN special has diluted statistics of the education of Blacks in America. By focusing on an Achievement Gap between black and white children, misses the achievement of black children as a whole. Instead of displaying the obvious, they should have put more focus on the unseen. Then the existence of the draining of the urban public schools of their more advance students sending them to more advance rural schools via vouchers, and leaving the urban public school struggling to maintain with average or less than average students and funding. Rural schools are becoming overcrowded and urban schools are chasing dropouts to re-register; creating alternative programs to prevent increasing dropout rates, all to get more funding to better teach the remaining students and avoid closure. There was an in depth study of a particular school system in the Baltimore, Maryland area that concluded this same result.

Overstating problems of being Black in America without solutions is no more than what many former Civil Rights Leaders have done, many of whom were looking for no more than sound-bite opportunities, is what I hope would not be all that would have been accomplished in this series. I truly hope that the new non-traditional politicians heed the covert call to action.

"Blacks are more likely than whites to die from cancer, strokes, asthma and heart disease." Mainstream Media would have you believe that the results are higher through crime and violence. It was reported in this special, due to lack of proper healthcare accessibility, stress and poverty we are subject to be apart of the aforementioned statistics. Now, tell me something I did not know. This issue is no longer just an African American issue; the issue is similar today, affecting more of our counterparts as well. WAKE UP EVERYBODY...NO MORE SLEEPING IN BED and you know the rest of that song recorded by Harold Melvin and the Bluenotes featuring Teddy Pendergrass. Never mind Community Health Fairs, we need more Community Health Clinics in our communities.

What I found to be alarming is that mainstream media is not speaking of the steady increase of black households to the middleclass society. According to the Pew

Research Center in 2006, 32% of black households had an income of at least $50,000 compared to 18% in 1970. What is so alarming is that mainstream media only report the stats of the crime rate in the urban areas. Which I believe to be exaggerated, I truly believe that crime rate is either lower or about the same when compared to the black households crossing out of poverty. What I also find alarming is the existence of such a thin line between lower class society and the middle class society, that at any given time that black household bringing in $50,000 can also be considered as the upper lower instead of the bottom middle if these figures are adjusted for inflation.

As I completed watching the entire two part series, I could not help but get angered at Joseph C. Phillips remarks, because he has not experienced racism, YET...does not mean it does not exist. I myself did not experienced racism until just recently. I am obligated by law not to discuss this issue being that there is an ongoing investigation by the federal government. In regard to Mr. Phillip's remarks: "of no innocent people in jail." My only question to him is what is the alternative? Don't do the crime...then what should they do to survive? This is not to excuse the criminals in our prison system; it however, is just to reinforce my feelings that we should not be so judgmental towards any race, especially the white race. They have done no more to us, then what we have and are doing to ourselves. If we are not offering an extended hand of help; just a judgmental finger pointing...remember there remains three pointed back at you. So SHUT UP! All in all, I think, although it was a bit informative in some aspects, it dropped the ball when no information as to how we as black in America is dealing on a political level. This disappointment brings me to other disappointments in my life.

The Years of Disappointments

As I watch the CNN special I also reminisced on my elementary and junior high school experiences. The life of Kenneth Allen is what came closest to my life experience. To be told by a teacher to consider a different career path, this was committed to him by a white teacher, but what happens when it's a black teacher? I started school a year early and was left back. Not because of academics, but because of social issues. My parents wanted me to be with children my age. Could you imagine the embarrassment of being held back in first grade?

I recalled being vetted to join the varsity basketball team at the Catholic Elementary School that I was attending by a black coach. With three brothers and three sisters, my father wanting to be more independent, and refused his mother and father financial help in raising his children. With the cost of tuition, uniforms, books and supplies for two children; he was the sole bread winner. I was transferred to a public junior high school, and decided to try out for that team, I was devastated when my name was called to perform certain drills and just walking past the coach, and I had not even touched the ball. Hearing the coach say, "you will never play professional ball with those small ankles." This statement was made by an African American man, a man whom was not only the coach, but a physical education teacher as well as the boy's Dean. However, I gave a half hearted attempt at performing his drills and left the gym.

I went home and did not tell a soul about this, I often wondered what my father would have said, if I had told him about this. Would that conversation change the outcome of my life and just what would I be doing today? The next day despite the lackluster performance I gave, to my amazement I had made it to the next round of eliminations. I was ashamed and still feeling rejection. I decided not to go to the next practice; instead I started hanging out with the wrong crowd. This team won the championship that year and the star player, (Gary Springer) went on to bring a championship to his high school team, (Benjamin Franklin High School) and received a scholarship to Syracuse University. He was later recruited and played with the Philadelphia 76ers. Time was taken with this young man at an early age by the same coach who told me "I would never make it." I wonder if I had attended that next practice and put forth my best effort, would I have had the opportunity to play alongside Gary Springer? Would that coach have taken the same time with me? Would I have proven this coach wrong? If I had it to do over again, I would change very little in my life, but this is one. I would have talked to my father, I am sure that this would have opened a special bond between us, if nothing else.

I became class president in my junior high school; this was more a popularity contest and not anything political. However, it did start my development of leadership qualities. I had started skipping classes. I spent that time in the school library, reading History books. It was not long before I was skipping school altogether. I spent that time riding the city bus to the last stop reading my school books, library books and any book that peaked my interest. I was held back again. My first girlfriend was an Honor Roll student at an all girl's private High School. She was a young protégé of sorts. I remember skipping school to hang out in the smoking bathroom at her school. Eventually I was caught in the bathroom and the Dean demanded that I tell on the people I was supposedly visiting and I refused to answer. I was told to leave the school and never return or I would be charged with trespassing. I had failed this year and to repeat the seventh grade. I finally made it to the eighth grade where I was sent on to High School. I started hanging with an older crowd; it was not long before I dropped out of high school in the ninth grade. this was done to avoid repeating the ninth grade and becoming three years behind.

My next major disappointment came at age 17; I had enlisted in the United States Army. I went through basic training, in Fort Jackson, SC. I truly felt for a young man whom had never been away from home I was an average soldier. There was some discipline problems and eventually I was discharged. While other comrades were marching on the parade field for graduation from basic training, I was marching trough the Reception Center completing separation papers. I was told that my discharge was under honorable conditions and that I had to wait two years before I could reenlist. I was given a RE-3 reenlistment code. Unaware of what this meant at the time, but fully made aware of three years later when I tried to get back in. It was explained to me by an Army Recruiter that there was a digit missing from the reenlistment code on my DD-214. After sending and waiting nearly six months for a new DD-214 with the entire reenlistment code. To my amazement I found out that I was labeled as "unable to adapt to military life." and given a RE-3C code. During my short stint in the Army, I was given a verbal counseling for buying a Pepsi cola while under restriction. I say buying because the Pepsi Cola was confiscated by the Watch Commander and I never drunk the soda.

I was also given a verbal counseling for using the payphone while on restriction. How was these two verbal counseling constitute an inability to adapt to military life. I guess you are saying why was I was on restriction in these cases. All recruits at that time were on restriction during basic training. I needed the equivalent of an act of congress to get back in the Army.

These three major disappointments along with a few other minor ones, led me down a path of cocaine and alcohol addiction I call my rebellious years.

The Rebellious Years

During these years I had done a great deal of things that I am ashamed of especially the brief, separation from my wife and family. However, I am grateful to those things I saw and learned about myself; the people I met and places visited. I was still hanging out with an older crowd during junior high school. I started going through my rebellion. I was eventually introduced to cocaine at age 18. My years of rebellion were not that of an average teen that was wild and unstable and oftentimes a bit dangerous. My rebellion was more of calculated, strategic risks with very little danger. My rebellion can be considered more of a learning experience. When I was told I couldn't, I figured out a way to do it. I was taught the laws and rules of the street by people of the street. Number one rule of the street is never show fear. I then adopted the term of "never let them see you sweat." And I still practice this today.

My first job came at age 17 right after my return from the Army. I got the job through my father, as a Night Porter in a Harlem Office Building. I was making $15.00 an hour at first, six months later I joined the Union and was then making about $19.50 an hour. Quite a bit of money but was not a job I wanted to spend my life doing. I eventually received a job in a savings bank and met the woman whom would later become my wife and the mother of my children. We had a medium size, traditional, Catholic style wedding. A few years later I lost my mother and the pain of that loss is truly indescribable. Though I knew no one could replace the love of your mother. I was in search for it none the less, and thought I had found it in Cocaine. Cocaine had deluded my thinking altogether. Cocaine and alcohol addiction led me to a stint in a homeless shelter; a break up of my marriage; in-patient and out-patient substance abuse treatment programs. I remember the despair of living in that shelter in Brooklyn, New York. It had been nicknamed "Castle Grey Skull." The Atlantic Avenue Men's Shelter, I had a cot in the Drug Free Dorm, or what I called the Free Drug Dorm. Illegal drugs and their use were rampant in this part of the shelter. I thought that I would be safe as I set out my journey of treatment. I could not believe the way these drugs were getting into the dorm. I thought that all in this dorm was in recovery, but soon found out that most were low level drug dealers. They were being paid with drugs and alcohol, instead of money. I was totally amazed at how this contraband ended up in the dorm. Majority of these men were recently released from prison. They had no vocational or academic education. Many of them conjured up schemes and other crimes to commit.

This stay lasted three long weeks; I was so relieved when I finally received a bed in Phoenix House. This set me on a journey of recovery. I detoured from the usual path of recovery but eventually found an out-patient program, which dealt with addiction in a physical, spiritual, mental, social, economical and political way. Allowing for all involve becoming productive members of society. I am truly grateful for the process of resocialization and reconciliation. Resocialization process through Phase: Piggy Back, Inc. Reconciliation process: with the God of my understanding; with myself; with my wife and family.

As a Striver in this program, I became politically active by becoming the president of the Striver's Committee; my political career became apparent to me. We raised enough money to charter a bus to take 48 recovering substance abusers to a

National Convention of Narcotics Anonymous for the day. I was given the opportunity to meet the Hon. Charles Rangel and former Drug Scar Gen. Barry McCaffrey and to state our protest at the reduction of funding for Substance Abuse Programs. I received a compliment about my speaking ability, from the Hon. Charles Rangel, and this was the start of my political aspirations. I must state that I was a member of the Independent Party. I became an Independent at first because of an attraction for Dr. Lenora Fulani. She being several years my senior, I licked my wounds of disappointment, and moved on. This led me to get into the history of the Democratic and Republican parties. What I found out about these major parties and the research of the Independent party of New York of course made me a proud card carrying member.

Spiritually speaking I ran a gambit. I started in Catholicism then converted to Baptist; then joined the Nation of Islam; then converted to Sunni Orthodox Islam; I then converted back to Baptist and finally now I consider myself to be a non-denominational Christian. I became a licensed Baptist minister at Greater Calvary Baptist Church; in Harlem, NY and under then Pastor Roger E. Watkins. I am currently a proud member of St. Paul's Baptist Church; in Henrico County, VA and under the current Senior Pastor Lance Watson.

Becoming Political Aware

The Independent Years

In 1985, I was quite the rebel, and joined the New Alliance Party. The New Alliance Party (NAP) was an American political party formed in New York City in 1979. The Nap's first chairperson was then-South Bronx City Councilman Gilberto Gerena-Valentin, a veteran Puerto Rican political activist. The party is notable for getting African

American psychologist Lenora Fulani on the ballot in all 50 states during her first Presidential campaign in 1988, making her both the first African-American and woman to do so. In 1984 the NAP made its entry into the Presidential campaign scene. Its candidate was Dennis L. Serrette, an African-American union activist who would later leave the NAP alleging questionable methods used by Newman and others. Serrette's running mate was Nancy Ross, a NAP leader who had served on a community school board on Manhattan's Upper West Side.

NAP began its unusual political "relationship" with Jesse Jackson. While Newman was initially dismissive of Jackson, Fulani had praised the popular activist during his 1984 Presidential run. After Jackson founded his Rainbow Coalition group, Newman and Fulani created the Rainbow Alliance, which at first lobbied for the benefit of small political parties. It later changed its name to the Rainbow Lobby and expanded its lobby to include issues of opposing U.S.-backed Joseph Mobutu's dictatorship in Zaire and the Haitian dictatorship of Prosper Avril. When asked about his political relationship to Fulani in the press Jackson said that there was no relationship at all. The Rainbow Lobby continued its lobbying activities into the early 1990s, while Fulani repeatedly rebuked Jackson for his support of the Democratic Party.

The 1988 presidential race was a major step for the NAP. The Fulani campaign ran under the slogan "Two Roads are Better than One," supporting Reverend Jesse Jackson's campaign within the Democratic Party while launching her own run designed to challenge the African American community to sever their historic relationship to the Democratic Party and embrace an independent path. In the previous election, NAP was able to secure a ballot spot in only 33 states. This time around NAP pursued every avenue possible to gain ballot access. This included attempts to gain the nomination of small independent parties which existed around the country, such as the Solidarity Party in Illinois. Fulani had six different running mates; different ones in different states, among them Joyce Dattner and (in Oregon only) Harold Moore, each "representing different constituencies." Asked which one would become Vice President if she won, she answered "If we got elected, we'd figure it out." Fulani's vote total throughout the country was 217,221, or 0.2% of the vote, coming in fourth place. She was the second most successful third party presidential candidate that year, behind Libertarian Ron Paul. In the 1988 election, the NAP ran some candidates for other offices, including US Senate candidates in Connecticut, Massachusetts, Pennsylvania and Nebraska. Though the party had its strongest roots in the east coast, the best result for the NAP was in Nebraska, where they had a well-known candidate in independent state senator Ernie Chambers who received 1.6% of the vote.

Fulani ran unsuccessfully as a New York gubernatorial candidate in 1990. She was endorsed by Nation of Islam leader Minister Louis Farrakhan, who had recently been politically involved with Jesse Jackson's 1988 campaign only to be dropped at the recommendation of Jackson's campaign advisors. This was in the wake of Farrakhan being characterized in the press as anti-Semitic, as well Jackson's slipped comment of calling New York City "Hymietown." Fulani and Newman embraced Farrakhan, eliciting the anger of the Anti-Defamation League (ADL). In the wake of this criticism, Fulani moderated a "historic conference" on Black-Jewish relations, featuring the "Jewish Marxist" Newman dialoguing with activist Reverend Al Sharpton.

Fulani again ran for president in 1992 on the NAP ticket. Maria Elizabeth Muñoz, a chicano activist, was chosen as her running mate. Muñoz had previously run for Senate and Governor in California on Peace and Freedom Party tickets. Fulani lost the party's nomination to Ron Daniels of Jesse Jackson's Rainbow Coalition. She also entered the New Hampshire primary for the Democratic Party Presidential nomination in 1992, and gained some press coverage for frequent heckling of Bill Clinton's campaign appearances after she was excluded from the New Hampshire Democratic debates. In 1992, the NAP also ran some candidates in other races, including US Senate candidates in Arizona, Illinois, Indiana and New York. The best result for NAP Senate candidates was for Mohammad T. Mehdi in New York, who received 0.8% of the vote and fourth place.

By the mid 1990s the NAP and its weekly newspaper The National Alliance had been disbanded. In 1994, Fulani and Newman for a period joined the Patriot Party, one of many groups which would later compete for control over Ross Perot's Reform Party in the years to come. This same year, Fulani and former National Alliance editor Jacqueline Salit formed the Committee for a Unified Independent Party, an organization dedicated to bringing various independent groups together to challenge the bipartisan nature of American politics.

I followed the political activity of Dr. Fulani as she made history, something that has not been recognized as she should. She also received the most votes for a woman for President in a United States General Election. I was very much persuaded by her political concerns of racial equality and political reform. In 2000, years after leaving the NAP I took a hiatus from political organizations. I had reconciled with my wife and family; we moved to Tuscaloosa, Alabama. After spending a few months there we moved to

Norfolk, Virginia, and I began looking for an Independent Political Organization and after moving to Richmond, we found the Independent Greens of Virginia.

The Independent Greens of Virginia, (also known as the Indy Greens), is the state affiliate of the Independence Party of America in the Commonwealth of Virginia. It became a state party in 2003 from a division of the Green Party of Virginia. When the state meeting of the Green Party of Virginia refused to recognize Carey Campbell's installation as chair of the Arlington Chapter of the GPVA and subsequently disaffiliated the chapter and expelled Campbell from the party, Campbell and Joe Oddo then formed a new statewide party.

The party, separate from the national Green Party, affiliated itself with the Independence Party of America on January 10, 2008. The platform of the Independent Greens focuses on fiscal conservatism, as well transportation issues, running on the slogans "Fiscally Conservative, Socially Responsible" and "More Trains, Less Traffic."

The Indy Greens started in the Virginia Independent tradition of Harry F. Byrd Jr. of Winchester, Virginia. He was the second Independent elected to the United States Senate in American history.

In their original party plan, platform and bylaws, Indy Greens described themselves as a "values conservative party." The phrase came from Petra Kelly, and co-author the Christian conservative Herbert Gruehl in their original Green Party platform.

Like Senator Byrd, the Indy Greens called for balanced budgets at local, state, and federal levels, and paying off the federal debt. As with Petra Kelly's original Green Party platform that called for rotation/term limits, Indy Greens advocate term limits.

From the start these activist were dedicated to "More candidates, less apathy."which means working with all independents, and third parties to put more candidates on the ballot. This organization was where I launched my political career. I ran for Virginia's 74th District State House Delegate.

The Indy Greens encourage all citizens to run for office, as a form of civic responsibility: "More candidates, less apathy." Any qualified candidate can run under the party label; candidates are taken on "first come, first served" basis. The party's goal is to offer voters a positive alternative on the ballot, by permitting average citizens to run for office. The campaigns are intended to be grassroots-financed and run. The strategy of running candidates in every means political strength and growth are come from being on the ballot. Indy Green strategy has the advantage of combining efforts in every aspect of campaigning.

I became disenchanted with The Independence Party because of the Party's platform is somewhat ambiguous. The party itself is designed to draw independent voters. The IGVA is the only party in the United States that allows non-affiliated voters to vote in its primary elections. Most often, it chooses a candidate who will draw the party the most votes, either by using electoral fusion or by picking someone who has significant name recognition (for instance, an incumbent who was ousted in a primary election).

I however, owe a bit of gratitude to the current Chairman Carey Campbell and the other leaders of the Independent Greens of Virginia for the experience I obtain from them.

What is a Democrat?

The Democratic Party is one of two or three major political parties in the United States, (depending on your perspective) the other being the Republican Party and the Independent Party. The Democratic Party is the oldest political party in continuous operation in the United States and is one of the oldest parties in the world.

The Democratic Party traces its origins to the Democratic-Republican Party, founded by Thomas Jefferson, James Madison and other influential opponents of the Federalists Party in 1712. However, the modern Democratic party truly arose in the 1830's, with the election of Andrew Jackson.

In 2004, it was the largest political party, with 77 million voters (42.6% of 169 million registered) claiming affiliation. An August 2008 estimate is that 51% of registered voters, including Independents, lean toward the Democratic Party, 38% lean toward the Republican Party and the remainder expresses no preference.

Historically, the party has favored farmers, laborers, labor unions, religious and ethnic minorities; it has opposed unregulated business and finance, and favored progressive income taxes. In the 1930's, the party began advocating welfare spending programs targeted at the poor. The party had a pro-business wing; typified by Al Smith, that shrank in the 1930's, and a Southern conservative wing that shrank after President Lyndon B. Johnson supported the Civil Rights Act of 1964.

In recent decades, the party has adopted a centrist economic and more socially progressive agenda, with the voter base having shifted considerably. Once dominated by unionized labor and the working class, the Democratic base now consists of social liberals who tend to be well-educated as well as the socially more conservative working class.

From the end of the Civil War, African Americans favored the Republican Party. However, they began drifting to the Democratic Party in the 1930's, as Franklin Roosevelt's New Deal programs gave economic relief to all minorities, including African Americans and Hispanics. Support for the Civil Rights Movement in the 1960s by Lyndon B. Johnson helped give the Democrats even larger support among the African American community, that's of course, after the untimely death of John F. Kennedy, although their position also alienated the Southern whites population and led to a split in the parties, with most liberals going to the Democratic Party and most conservatives, such as the "Dixiecrats" moving towards the Republican Party.

Now, I must admit that I nearly was duped into becoming a Republican, Since the September 11, 2001 attacks, the party supports neoconservative policies with regard to the "War on Terror." including the 2001 war in Afghanistan and the 2003 invasion of Iraq. It was the invasion of Iraq that brought me back to my senses. In any event here is the information on the other party.

The Republican Party was created in 1854 in opposition to the Kansas-Nebraska Act that would have allowed the expansion of slavery into Kansas. Besides opposition to slavery, the new party put forward a progressive vision of modernizing the United States: emphasizing higher education; banking; railroads; industry and cities, while promising free homesteads to farmers. Its initial base was in the Northeast and Midwest. The Party nominated Abraham Lincoln and ascended to power in the election of 1860. The party fought for the Union in the American Civil War and presided over Reconstruction. The party rejected Lincoln for the election of 1864. Lincoln ran under the National Union Party. The Republican Party restarted in 1869. The party's success spawned factionalism within the party in the 1870s. Those disturbed by Ulysses S. Grant ran Horace Greeley for the presidency against him. The Stalwarts defended the spoils system; the Half-Breeds pushed for reform of the civil service.

The GOP supported big business generally, hard money (i.e., the gold standard), high tariffs, and generous pensions for Union veterans, and the annexation of Hawaii. The Republicans supported the Protestants who demanded Prohibition. As the Northern post-bellum economy boomed with heavy and light industry, railroads, mines, fast-growing cities and prosperous agriculture, the Republicans took credit and promoted policies to sustain the fast growth. But by 1890, the Republicans had agreed to the Sherman Antitrust Act and the Interstate Commerce Commission in response to complaints from owners of small businesses and farmers. The high McKinley Tariff of 1890 hurt the party and the Democrats swept to a landslide in the off-year elections, even defeating McKinley himself.

After the two terms of Democrat Grover Cleveland, the election of William McKinley in 1896 is widely seen as a resurgence of Republican dominance and is sometimes cited as a realigning election. McKinley promised that high tariffs would end the severe hardship caused by the Panic of 1893, and that the GOP would guarantee a sort of pluralism in which all groups would benefit. The Republicans were cemented as the party of business, though mitigated by the succession of Theodore Roosevelt who embraced trust-busting. He later ran of a third party ticket of the Progressive Party and challenged his previous successor William Howard Taft. The party controlled the presidency throughout the 1920s, running on a platform of opposition to the League of Nations, high tariffs, and promotion of business interests. Warren G. Harding, Calvin Coolidge and Herbert Hoover were resoundingly elected in 1920, 1924, and 1928 respectively. The Teapot Dome scandal threatened to hurt the party but Harding died and Coolidge blamed everything on him, as the opposition splintered in 1924. The pro-business policies of the decade seemed to produce an unprecedented prosperity, until the Wall Street Crash of 1929 heralded the Great Depression.

The second half of the 20th century saw election of Republican presidents Dwight D. Eisenhower, Richard Nixon, Ronald Reagan, George H. W. Bush, and George W. Bush. The Republican Party, led by House Republican Minority Whip Newt Gingrich campaigning on a Contract with America, was elected to majorities to both houses of Congress in the Republican Revolution of 1994. Their majorities were generally held until the Democrats regained control in the mid-term election of 2006. In the 21st century the Republican Party is defined by social conservatism, an aggressive foreign policy attempting to defeat terrorism and promote global democracy, a more powerful executive branch, tax cuts, and deregulation and subsidization of industry.

The voter base of the Republican Party is as follows:

Business community: The GOP is usually seen as the traditionally pro-business party and it garners major support from a wide variety of industries from the financial sector to small businesses. This may relate to the fact that Republicans are about 50% more likely to be self-employed and are more likely to work in the area of management.
Gender: Since 1980 a "gender gap" has seen slightly stronger support for the GOP among men than among women. In the 2006 House races, 43% of women voted for GOP, while 47% of men did so.
Race: Since 1964, the GOP has been weakly represented among African Americans, winning under 15% of the black vote in recent national elections (1980 to 2004). The party has recently nominated African American candidates for senator or governor in Illinois, Ohio, Pennsylvania and Maryland, though none were successful. The Republican Party supported the abolition of slavery under Abraham Lincoln, and from the Civil War

until the Great Depression of the 1930s, blacks voted for Republican candidates by an overwhelming margin; in the Southern states, they were often not allowed to vote, but received Federal patronage appointments from the Republicans. The majority of black Americans switched to the Democratic Party in the 1930s when the New Deal offered them governmental support for civil rights. In recent decades, the party has been more successful in gaining support from Hispanic and Asian American voters than from African Americans. George W. Bush, who campaigned significantly for Hispanic votes, received 35% of their vote in 2000 and 44% in 2004. In 2004, 44% of Asian Americans voted for Bush. The party's strong anti-communist stance has made it popular among some minority groups from current and former Communist states, in particular Cuban Americans and Vietnamese Americans. In the 2006 House races, the GOP won 51% of white votes, 37% of Asian votes, and 30% of Hispanic votes, while winning only 10% of African American votes. For decades, a greater percentage of Caucasian voters self-identified as Democrats, rather than Republicans. However, since the mid-1990s whites have been more likely to self-identify as Republicans than Democrats.

Family status: In recent elections, Republicans have found their greatest support among whites from married couples with children living at home. Unmarried and divorced women were far more likely to vote for Kerry in 2004.

Income: Poorer voters tend favor the Democratic Party while wealthier voters tend to support the Republican Party. Bush won 41% of the poorest 20% of voters in 2004, 55% of the richest 20%, and 53% of those in between. In the 2006 House races, the voters with incomes over $50,000 were 49% Republican, while those under were 38%.

Military: Republicans hold a large majority in the armed services, with 57% of active military personnel and 66% of officers identified as Republican in 2003.

Education: Self-identified Republicans are significantly more likely than Democrats to have 4-year college degrees. Regarding graduate-level degrees (master's or doctorate), there exist a rough parity between Democrats and Republicans. According to the Gallup Organization: "Both Democrats and Republicans have equal numbers of Americans at the upper end of the educational spectrum that is, with post graduate degrees." Republicans remain a small minority in academia, with 15% of full-time faculty identifying as conservative.

Age: The Democrats do better among younger Americans and Republicans among older Americans. In 2006, the GOP won only 38% of the voters aged 18-29.

Sexual Orientation: Exit polls conducted in 2000, 2004 and 2006 indicate that 23-25% of gay and lesbian Americans voted for the GOP. In recent years, the party has opposed same-sex marriage, adoption by same-sex couples, inclusion of sexual orientation in hate crimes laws, the Employment Non-Discrimination Act, while supporting the use of the "Don't ask, don't" tell policy within the military. The opposition to gay rights found in the Republican Party largely comes from the very religious and socially conservative portion of the party.

Religion. Religion has always played a major role for both parties but, in the course of a century, the parties' religious compositions have changed. Religion was a major dividing line between the parties before 1960, with Catholics, Jews, and Southern Protestants heavily Democratic, and Northeastern Protestants heavily Republican. Most of the old differences faded away after the realignment of the late 1960s that undercut the New Deal coalition.

Region: Since 1980, geographically the Republican "base" ("red states") is strongest in the South and West, and weakest in the Northeast and the Pacific Coast. The Northeast does well for the GOP in state contests but not in presidential ones (except New Hampshire). The Midwest has been roughly balanced since 1854, with Illinois becoming more Democratic due to the City of Chicago and Minnesota and Wisconsin more Republican since 1990. Since the 1930s the Democrats have dominated most central cities, the Republicans now dominate rural areas, and the majority of suburbs.

Conservatives and Moderates: The Republican coalition is quite diverse, and numerous factions compete to frame platforms and select candidates. The "conservatives" are strongest in the South, where they draw support from religious conservatives. The "moderates" tend to dominate the party in New England, and used to be well represented in all states.

The future trends according to Republican Karl Rove and other commentators had speculated about a permanent political realignment in favor of the GOP along the lines of the presidential election of 1896, in which Mark Hanna helped William McKinley construct a Republican majority that lasted for the next 36 years. While the American political sphere is relatively evenly divided in terms of ideology, the Republican Party trails the Democrats by 17 million registered members. Skeptics ask if the Republican Party can simultaneously contain both libertarians and social conservatives, or if it can contain a business community that may use illegal immigrants as employees, and Hispanic voters.

Republican optimists also point to the success of Roosevelt's Democratic coalition, which held together even more disparate elements. Until 2007, the Republican Party has remained fairly cohesive, as both strong economic libertarians and strong social conservatives are opposed to the Democrats, who they see as both the party of bigger and more secular, progressive government. Yet, libertarians are increasingly dissatisfied with the party's social policy and support for corporate welfare and national debt, which some believe has grown increasingly restrictive of personal liberties, and with the Bush

Administration greatly increasing the federal debt. Some social conservatives are also growing increasingly dissatisfied with the party's support for economic policies that they see as contradictory to their moral values. Presidential candidate Mike Huckabee has remarked that "If it was all about the money ... then we might as well put the presidency up on eBay."

Webster's definition of a democrat is a person concerned with individual rights and liberties; social equality and respect; tend to be anti-big business; in favor of tax increases, government intervention, and government programs, and favor the rules of the majority. This leads me to why I'm an Independent Democrat.

Why I am a Blue Dog Conservative Democrat

Political ideologies in the United States vary considerably. People in the U.S. generally classify themselves either as adhering to American Liberalism, American Conservatism or as Moderates. The ideological position a person or party takes may be described in terms of social and economic policy. The ideological positions a person assumes on social and economic policy issues may differ in their position on the political spectrum. With over 72 million registered members, the Democratic Party is home to an ideologically diverse base. Liberals form, by far the largest and most influential ideological demographic within the party.

Social liberals also referred to as progressives or modern liberals, constitute a large part of the Democratic voter base. Liberals thereby form the largest united typographical demographic and now comprise perhaps the most vital component within the Democratic base. A majority of liberals favor diplomacy over military action, stem cell research, the legalization of same-sex marriage, secular government, stricter gun control, and environmental protection laws as well as the preservation of abortion rights. Immigration and cultural diversity is deemed positive; liberals favor cultural pluralism, a system in which immigrants retain their native culture in addition to adopting their new culture. They tend to be divided on free trade agreements and organizations such as the North American Free Trade Agreement.

Civil libertarians also often support the Democratic Party because Democratic positions on such issues as civil rights and separation of church and state are more closely aligned to their own than the positions of the Republican Party, and because the Democratic economic agenda may be more appealing to them than that of the Libertarian Party. They oppose gun control, the "War on Drugs," protectionism, corporate welfare, government debt, and an interventionist foreign policy.

Conservative Democrats represent 15% of registered voters and 14% of the general electorate. In the House of Representatives, the Blue Dog Coalition, a caucus of fiscal and social conservatives and moderates, primarily southerners, forms part of the Democratic Party's current faction of conservative Democrats. They have acted as a unified voting bloc in the past, giving its 40 plus members some ability to change legislation and broker compromises with the Republican Party's leadership. Pro-life Democrats are sometimes classified as conservatives on the basis of social conservatism.

Though centrist Democrats differ on a variety of issues, they typically foster a mix of political views and ideas. Compared to other Democratic factions, they are tend to be more supportive of the military use of force, including the war in Iraq, and are more willing to reduce government welfare, as indicated by their support for welfare reform and tax cuts. One of the most influential factions is the Democratic Leadership Council

(DLC), a nonprofit organization that advocates centrist positions for the party. The DLC hails President Bill Clinton as proof of the viability of "Third Way" politicians and a DLC success story. Former Representative Harold Ford, Jr. of Tennessee is its current chairman.

Since I ideally fit in with each of these factions, this is why I consider myself an Independent Democrat. If I was solely committed to any one faction of the Democratic Party, it would have to be the Blue Dog Coalition. I do differ with them on their support of certain issues, but all in all we should all be very fiscal conservative in our ideals. As an Independent Democrat, (or Blue Dog Democrat) allows me the freedom to support other views and puts me in a position to reach those Independents voters as well as the disappointed Republican voters. This also allows me the opportunity to reach across to the other side of the aisle and finally help put an end to the gridlock in congress.

The courage to run

Traditional Politician

These people cannot be politicians! They don't look like politicians, they don't dress like politicians, they don't eat like politicians, they don't act like politicians, and they don't even have politician names. Where are the politicians who look like politicians?

This comment was made by a local district politician following a focus group meeting, and dinner of community organizers. His view of politicians is shared by most people who are not apart of this new Middle Class in America. They think politicians are big name lawyers, ex-judges, former corporate executives with expensive clothes, watches, cars and eat in upscale restaurants. We have found this not to be the case.

Portrait of a Non-Traditional Politician

As a matter of fact this new politician would be found in his element at a neighborhood cookout or fish fry, arriving in a Dodge Caliber, dressed in a linen leisure suit sporting a Fossil. He would rather be eating sautéed scallops and not caviar; raw clams on the half shell and not sushi; a "pimp steak" and not filet mignon. You might find him on line at a local "McDonald's" or "Popeye's." This new politician is literally "of the people." He will not be making sound bites of party platform issues; he will only discuss the issues that concern the people and their resolve because he's literally "for the people." He is only waiting to be placed in a position to affect necessary change "by the people."

Traditional politician normally during a primary election stick to one particular side of an issue—gun control, the death penalty for child rapists and domestic wiretapping—and moves to the center during the general election. This "flip-flopping' is prevalent on both sides, giving the voter impression that a typical politician would say anything to get elected. This 'flip-flopping' displays a lack of integrity, which is a characteristic that most people expect of typical politicians. Oftentime excused because of being typical political rhetoric. Lawyers often hide behind the Hippocratic Oath in order to justify this lack of integrity. They tend to rely on the apathetic voter to further advance their selfish view of certain issues. When asked to describe a politician in general, people tend to give a description that would make the average person ashamed to be associated with any politician. With that said just who would even consider a career in politics?

With the depth of political corruption and other scandals the portrait of a typical politician is similar to that of a typical crook. Sex, power and money are usually at the root of these scandals. Where is the integrity, morals and values of the typical politician? Not all politicians fit in the usual portrait by most citizens. Media coverage plays a big factor in the way most people shape their opinion and views about a typical politician. When these scandals become headlines, a vast majority of people are often shocked, but then there exist the others who will say "I knew he was crooked all the time!" How and where to start, to change that portrait?

Politician Defined

A vast majority of definitions give a derogatory look at the political system as a whole. Depending on the source, the existence of numerous definitions, although similar in substance the difference is in the tone. Let us take a look at a few of them:

Dictionary.com: a seeker or holder of public office, who is more concerned about winning favor or retaining power than maintaining principles.

American Heritage Dictionary: one who seeks personal or partisan gain, often by scheming and maneuvering?

Webster's II New College Dictionary: one who seeks personal or partisan gain, often by crafty or dishonest means.

Merriam Webster Dictionary: a person primarily interested in political office for selfish or other narrow usually shortsighted reasons.

These definitions fall in line with the average citizens thinking of typical politicians, thereby creating what we now regard as the traditional politician.

Non-traditional Politician

Unlike their traditional counterpart, the non-traditional politician is not a graduate of an Ivy League Law School. This is not to say they are uneducated, just a different type of education. The non-traditional politician may not be a college graduate at all. Their education often time is practical knowledge and life experience. This new politician can be little more than a high school graduate and self taught politically speaking via C-Span.

The non-traditional politician is not from the upper class society and does not strive to be apart of that world. Instead they are apart of the working middleclass society and often time at that lower end of that society. Just a paycheck away from: bankruptcy, the upper lower class society and poverty. The non-traditional politician understands the concept of living paycheck to paycheck, as they survive from paycheck to paycheck. Believe me a difference does exist, and if you know the difference then you are either a non-traditional politician or someone a non-traditional politician needs: a non-traditional voter.

The non-traditional politician was not "born with a silver spoon in their mouth." They had to earn all that they possess. In fact, they might have even been through bankruptcy. This was a situation that most would not want to be made public, but with the state of the economy today, it has become the norm. Bankruptcy is no longer a sign of incompetence but a learning experience. Who would have thought that one day bankruptcy would no longer be an embarrassment and become a fact of living life on life terms? Well this is part of the middle class society. Current bankruptcy laws were designed to stop the increase in bankruptcy filings. These laws are failing and millions of middle class society is suffering because of them.

The non-traditional politician does not believe that they must raise several hundred thousands of dollars to operate a successful campaign. In fact, they are quite frugal and believe in quality of money spent and not quantity. In point the responsibility now belongs to the non-traditional politician to change the perceptions and definitions of a politician.

Traditional vs. Non-traditional

"The definition of insanity is: repeating the same mistakes and expecting a different result." "Nothing Changes if Nothing Changes!"

The difficulty at this point is accurately to display an unbiased and bi-partisan comparison of traditional and non-traditional politicians. In doing so, I will "step outside the box," in order to accomplish this. As I am writing this book, we are within days of a history making Presidential Election. A black man is days away from being elected President of the United States. As I look back on the primaries both Democratic and Republican. We have a perfect example of traditional vs. non-traditional.

There were four non-traditional candidates in this year Presidential Primary Elections two were Democrats and two Republican: Senator Barack H. Obama (D) of Illinois; Senator Hillary R. Clinton (D) of New York and former Gov. Mitt Romney (R) of Massachusetts; former Gov. Michael D. Huckabee (R) of Arkansas. Sen. Obama is a black freshmen Senator; Sen. Clinton is a white woman in her second term and former First Lady; former Gov. Huckabee is a white Southern Baptist Minister and former Gov. Romney whom is a white man and a Mormon. On both sides of the aisle there also were the traditional white male candidates and on both sides it got ugly. I will give you a short version of the campaigns and bring it all up to date.

The scheming and maneuvering of all the candidates, (disguised as campaign tactics and strategies) was horrendous. Not to mention the money the Candidates have raised and are raising at this time. This election marks the first time since 1928 in which neither an incumbent President nor an incumbent Vice-President ran for their party's nomination. "Front runner" status is dependent on the news agency reporting, but by October 2007, the consensus listed about six candidates as leading the pack. For example, CNN listed Hillary Clinton, John Edwards, Rudolph Giuliani, Barack Obama, Fred Thompson, and Mitt Romney as the front runners. The Washington Post listed Clinton, Edwards and Obama as the Democratic frontrunners, "leading in polls and fundraising and well ahead of the other major candidates." MSNBC's Chuck Todd christened Giuliani and John McCain the Republican front runners after the second Republican presidential debate.

Between November 2006 and February 2007, eight major candidates opened their campaigns—Joe Biden, Hillary Clinton, Chris Dodd, John Edwards, Dennis Kucinich, Barack Obama, Bill Richardson, and Tom Vilsack—joining Mike Gravel, who had announced his candidacy in April 2006. Potential candidates John Kerry, Al Gore, Russ Feingold, Evan Bayh, Tom Daschle, Wesley Clark, Mark Warner, and Al Sharpton reportedly considered running but ultimately declined to seek the nomination. Vilsack dropped out in February 2007.

The reported cost of campaigning for President has increased significantly in recent years. One source reported that if the costs for both Democratic and Republican campaigns are added together (for the Presidential primary election, general election, and the political conventions) the costs have more than doubled in only eight years ($448.9

million in 1996, $649.5 million in 2000, and $1.01 billion in 2004). In January 2007, Federal Election Commission Chairman Michael E. Toner estimated the 2008 race will be a $1 billion election, and that to be taken seriously, a candidate needed to raise at least $100 million by the end of 2007.

Although he had said he would not be running for president, published reports indicated that billionaire and New York City mayor Michael Bloomberg had been considering a presidential bid as an independent with up to $1 billion of his own fortune to finance it. Bloomberg ultimately ended this speculation by unequivocally stating that he would not run. Had Bloomberg decided to run, he would not have needed to campaign in the primary elections or participate in the conventions, greatly reducing both the necessary length and cost of his campaign.

With the increase in money, the public financing system funded by the presidential election campaign fund check off has not been used by many candidates. John McCain, Tom Tancredo, John Edwards, Chris Dodd, and Joe Biden qualified for and elected to take public funds in the primary. Other major candidates eschewed the low amount of spending permitted, or gave other reasons as in the case of Barack Obama, and have chosen not to participate.

Howard Dean collected large contributions via the internet in his 2004 primary run. In 2008 candidates have gone even further in reaching out to Internet users through their own sites and through sites such as You Tube, My Space and Face Book. Republican Ron Paul and Democratic Party candidate Barack Obama have been the most active in courting voters through the Internet. On December 16, 2007, Ron Paul collected more money on a single day through Internet donations than any presidential candidate in

US history with over $6 million. Anonymous and semi-anonymous smear campaigns traditionally done with fliers and push calling have also spread to the Internet.

In the first three months of 2007, Clinton and Obama raised more than $20 million each and Edwards raised more than $12 million. The three candidates quickly became the frontrunners for the nomination, a status they held all the way through the end of 2007. At the end of the year, December 31, Clinton held a substantial lead in super delegates, and she was leading in the national polls with 42% of likely voters, over Obama, 23%, and Edwards, 16%. However, Edwards and Obama remained close in state polls for the early contests, including the Iowa caucuses, where the final polling average had Obama leading narrowly, 31%, over Clinton, 30%, Edwards, 26%, Biden, 5%, and Richardson, 5%.

Now, I believe if Sen. Clinton and Sen. Obama did not get caught up in the "Front Runner" status and teamed up at the start, this would have been an unbeatable ticket. It truly did not matter who was at the top of the ticket, this would have locked down the White House to the Democratic Party for at least 16 years. Especially if Sen. Clinton was at the top of the ticket for the first eight, Sen. Obama taken the second eight and his running mate being former Sen. John Edwards would have given the Democrats an additional eight years. But, as tradition would have it, it got ugly. Following tradition, the 2008 primary calendar began with the Iowa caucus and the New Hampshire primary. The Nevada caucus and the South Carolina primary were the third and fourth contests sanctioned by the Democratic National Committee. Under the national committee's rules, no state was allowed to hold primaries or caucuses before February 5 with the exceptions of these four states. Michigan and Florida also held early primaries, but as the contests were unsanctioned, the results were not recognized by the national committee until a political compromise was reached four months later.

Obama won the Iowa caucuses with 38% of the vote, over Edwards, 30%, and Clinton, 29%. His victory brought him to national prominence as many voters tuned in to the race for the first time. In a speech that evening, he defined change as the primary theme of his campaign and said, "On this January night, at this defining moment in history, you have done what the cynics said we couldn't do." The delegate count was virtually tied, but Clinton's surprising third-place finish in the popular vote damaged her image as the "inevitable" nominee. However, she remained upbeat, saying "This race begins tonight and ends when Democrats throughout America have their say. Our campaign was built for a marathon." The following day, reports described "panic" among some Clinton donors, and rumors of a staff shake-up began to circulate. Biden and Dodd withdrew from the race.

After Obama's upset win in Iowa, it appeared to many political observers that he would ride a wave of momentum through the New Hampshire primaries and onward to win the Democratic nomination. Eulogies were published on the Clinton campaign, as Obama surged to a roughly 10-point lead in the New Hampshire polls. However, the race turned quickly in the days before the primary, and the polls were slow to register a reversal toward Clinton. On January 5, Edwards sided with Obama against Clinton in a televised debate. In one noted exchange, Edwards said that Clinton could not bring about change, while he and Obama could: "Any time you speak out powerfully for change, the forces for status quo attack." Clinton passionately retorted, "Making change is not about what you believe; it's not about a speech you make. It's about working hard. I'm not just running on a promise for change. I'm running on 35 years of change. What we need is somebody who can deliver change. We don't need to be raising false hopes." It came to be seen as the defining statement for her candidacy. The morning before the primary, Clinton became "visibly emotional" in response to a friendly question from a voter. Video of the moment was replayed on cable news television throughout the day, accompanied by pundit commentary that ranged from sympathetic to callous in tone. Voters rallied to Clinton's defense, and she won a surprising three-percent victory over Obama in the popular vote. They tied in the delegate count. Richardson withdrew from the race on January 10.

Momentum shifted in Clinton's favor, and she won the popular vote in the Nevada caucuses 11 days later, despite Obama's endorsement from the influential Culinary Workers Union. However, Obama ran strongly in rural areas throughout the state and beat Clinton in the delegate count. Edwards's support collapsed in Nevada, as voters coalesced around the two apparent frontrunners. Dennis Kucinich withdrew from the race. In the following week, issues of race came to the fore as campaigning began for the South Carolina primary, the first to feature a large proportion of African Americans in the Democratic electorate. Behind in the state polls, Hillary Clinton left to campaign in some Super Tuesday states, while her husband, former president Bill Clinton, stayed in South Carolina and engaged in a series of exchanges with Obama. CBS News reported, "By injecting himself into the Democratic primary campaign with a series of inflammatory and negative statements, Bill Clinton may have helped his wife's presidential hopes in the long term but at the cost of his reputation with a group of voters African Americans that have long been one of his strongest bases of political support." Obama won by a more than two-to-one margin over Clinton, gaining 55% of the vote to her 27% and Edwards's 18%. The day of the primary, Bill Clinton compared Obama's expected win to Jesse Jackson's victory in the 1988 South Carolina primary. His comments were widely criticized as an apparent attempt to dismiss the primary results and marginalize Obama by implying that he was "the black candidate." The momentum generated by Obama's larger-than-expected win in South Carolina was deflated somewhat by the win Clinton claimed in the nullified Florida primary the following week. John Edwards suspended his candidacy on January 30. He did not immediately endorse either Clinton or Obama, but said they both had pledged to carry forward his central campaign theme of ending poverty in America. Neither Clinton nor Obama had a clear advantage heading into the Super Tuesday primaries, with 23 states and territories and 1,681 delegates at stake and more media attention than any primary election day in American history.

In August 2006, the Democratic National Committee adopted a proposal by its Rules and Bylaws Committee stating that only the four states of Iowa, New Hampshire, Nevada, and South Carolina would be permitted to hold primaries or caucuses before February 5, 2008. In May 2007, the Florida Legislature passed a bill that moved the date of the state's primary to January 29, 2008, setting up a confrontation with the DNC. In response, the DNC ruled that Florida's 185 pledged delegates and 26 super delegates would not be seated at the Democratic National Convention, or, if seated, would not be able to vote. In October 2007, Democrats from Florida's congressional delegation filed a federal lawsuit against the DNC to force recognition of its delegates, but the suit was unsuccessful. The presidential candidates promised not to campaign in Florida.

Meanwhile, Michigan moved its primary to January 15, 2008, also in violation of party rules. In October 2007, Obama, Richardson, Biden, and Edwards withdrew their names from the Michigan primary ballot, under pressure from the DNC and voters in Iowa and New Hampshire. Kucinich unsuccessfully sought to remove his name from the ballot, whereas Clinton and Dodd opted to remain on the ballot. In December 2007, the DNC ruled that Michigan's 128 pledged delegates and 29 super delegates would not count in the nominating contest unless it were held on a later date. The Michigan Democratic Party responded with a press release noting that the primary would proceed with Clinton, Dodd, Gravel, and Kucinich on the ballot. Supporters of Biden, Edwards, Richardson, and Obama were urged to vote "uncommitted" instead of writing in their candidates' names because write-in votes for those candidates would not be counted.

None of the top candidates campaigned in Florida or Michigan. The events were described in the media as "beauty contests," and voter turnout in both states was relatively low when compared with record-high turnout in other states. Nevertheless, Clinton claimed wins in Florida and Michigan, and she flew to Fort Lauderdale on the night of the Florida election to thank supporters for what she called a "tremendous victory." As the primaries continued, various groups tried to negotiate a resolution to the standoff between the DNC and the state parties. The Clinton campaign advocated first for the results to stand and for a new round of voting to take place in Michigan and Florida, while the Obama campaign deferred the matter to the DNC, while expressing a wish that the delegations be seated in some form. On all sides, Democrats worried that a failure to resolve the problem could lead to a rules or credential fight at the convention and low Democratic turnout in the general election in November. On May 31, 2008, the DNC

Rules and Bylaws Committee voted unanimously (27-0) to restore half-votes to all the Florida Delegates, including super delegates. The Michigan delegates were also given half-votes, with 69 delegates pledged to Hillary Clinton and 59 to Barack Obama; this proposed change passing by 19-8. The delegates will be so seated at the convention unless an appeal is subsequently filed with the Credentials Committee at the Convention itself, in Denver in late August.

Traditionally, "Super Tuesday" was the name given to the day on which the greatest number of States holding primary elections. In 2007, many states moved their primaries or caucuses early in the calendar to have greater influence over the race. As February 5 was the earliest date allowed by the Democratic National Committee, 23 states and territories moved their elections to that date. This year's Super Tuesday became the date of the nation's first quasi-national primary. It was dubbed "Super Duper Tuesday" or "Tsunami Tuesday," among other names.

After Obama's win in South Carolina on January 26, he received high-profile endorsements from Caroline Kennedy, daughter of former President John F. Kennedy, as well Senator Ted Kennedy, the former President's brother. Ted Kennedy's endorsement was considered "the biggest Democratic endorsement Obama could possibly get short of Bill Clinton or Al Gore." On January 31, Obama and Clinton met for the first time in a one-on-one debate, and they struck a friendly tone, seeking to put the racially-charged comments of the previous week behind them. Obama surged nationally in the polls and held campaign rallies that drew audiences of more than 15,000 people in several states.
A total of 1,681 pledged delegate votes were at stake in the states that voted on February 5. On election night, both Obama and Clinton claimed victories. In the popular vote,

Obama won 13 states and territories to Clinton's 10, including states like Idaho and Georgia where he won by very wide margins. His wins in Connecticut and Missouri were considered upsets.

However, Clinton won the large electoral prizes of California and Massachusetts, where some analysts had expected the Kennedy endorsements might carry Obama to victory. Although Obama gained significant ground from where he was polling in mid-January, it was not enough to close the gap in those states. In exit polls, Obama gained the overwhelming support of African American voters, and he strengthened his base among college-educated voters and voters younger than 45. Clinton found significant support among white women, Latinos, and voters over the age of 65. Obama ran strongest in caucus states, Rocky Mountain States, the South and the Midwest. Clinton ran strongest in the Northeast, the Southwest, and the states adjacent to Arkansas, where she served as first lady. When the delegate counting was finished, Obama won an estimated 847 pledged delegates to Clinton's 834. Early in the primary season, many observers had predicted that the nomination would be over after Super Tuesday, but the general verdict on election night was that the candidates had drawn to a virtual tie and that the race for the Democratic presidential nomination would not likely be settled for a month, at least.

In the following week, it became clear that a "tie" on Super Tuesday left Obama better positioned for the upcoming contests in February, where the demographics of several large states seemed to favor him. The day after Super Tuesday, February 6, Clinton announced that she had personally loaned her campaign $5 million in January. The news came as a surprise and set off another round of news stories about Clinton donors and supporters concerned about the campaign's strategy. It was particularly striking in contrast to Obama's announcement that he had raised a record-high $32 million in January, tapping 170,000 new contributors. It became clear that Obama's financial advantage had allowed him to organize and compete in a broader set of states on Super Tuesday, an advantage which was likely to continue in the coming weeks and months. Clinton's supporters responded by raising $6 million online in 36 hours, but Obama's campaign upped the ante, announcing their own total of $7.5 million in 36 hours and starting a new goal of reaching 500,000 new contributors in 2008 by the end of February.

As expected, Obama swept the three nominating events on February 9, which were thought to favor him based on the results in similar states that had voted previously. He then scored a convincing win in Maine, where Clinton had hoped to hold her ground. The same day, Clinton's campaign announced the resignation of campaign advisor Patti Solis Doyle. Obama's momentum carried through the following week, as he scored large delegate gains in the Potomac Primaries, taking the lead in the nationwide popular vote, even under the projection most favorable to Clinton, with Florida and Michigan included. NBC News declared him "Mr. Frontrunner" on February 13. Clinton attempted a comeback win in the demographically more favorable state of Wisconsin, but Obama won again by a larger margin than expected. In a span of 11 days, he swept 11 contests and extended his pledged delegate lead by 120. At the end of the month, Obama had 1,192 pledged delegates to Clinton's 1,035. He also began to close the gap in super delegates, although Clinton still led among super delegates, 240 to 191. Clinton's campaign tried to downplay the results of the February contests, and the candidate refused to acknowledge the losses in her speeches on election nights. Her advisers acknowledged that she would need big wins in the upcoming states to turn the race around.

With four states and 370 delegates at stake, March 4 was dubbed "Mini-Super Tuesday" or "Super Tuesday 2.0." Just as Obama had been favored in the mid-February states, Clinton was favored in Ohio, with its high proportion of working-class white voters and older voters, and Texas, with its high proportion of Latino voters. Exit polls in previous states showed that all three groups were a part of Clinton's base. In mid-February, Clinton held a 10-point lead in Texas and a 20-point lead in Ohio. The Clinton campaign set its sights on the Ohio-Texas "firewall," counting on a clear March 4 win to change the narrative and turn around her campaign for the nomination. Meanwhile, Obama hoped to score a win in one or both states that might be enough to knock Clinton out of the race. By February 25, they were in a statistical dead heat in Texas, according to a CNN poll.

In the last week of February, Clinton's campaign seemed to be back on its feet. A Saturday Night Live sketch mocked the media for its supposedly biased coverage in favor of Obama, and Clinton used the sketch to argue that Obama had not received proper scrutiny. The media responded by taking a more critical look at Obama's campaign. Meanwhile, Obama supporter and former fundraiser Tony Rezko went on trial in a political corruption case in Chicago. While Obama was not implicated, questions remained about how forthcoming he had been about his relationship with Rezko. Controversy also erupted when it was reported in the Canadian press that Obama economic advisor Austin Goolsbee had privately offered assurances that Obama's anti-

North American Free Trade Agreement rhetoric on the campaign trail was exaggerated. Obama's campaign denied the substance of the report, but their response was muddled by a series of missteps and may have hurt the candidate's standing with Ohio voters. Clinton launched a five-point attack on Obama's qualifications, "unleashing what one Clinton aide called a 'kitchen sink' fusillade," according to The New York Times. Perhaps the most damaging component was a campaign ad that aired in Texas, using the imagery of the White House "red phone" to suggest that Obama would not be prepared to handle a crisis as commander-in-chief when a phone call comes in to the White House at 3 a.m. The ad drew significant media attention in the four days before the election.

On election night, Clinton scored convincing wins in Ohio and Rhode Island. She narrowly won the Texas primary, while losing the Texas caucus. She pitched her wins that night as a comeback: "For everyone here in Ohio and across America who's ever been counted out but refused to be knocked out, and for everyone who has stumbled but stood right back up, and for everyone who works hard and never gives up, this one is for you." Obama focused on the "delegate math." He won the total delegate count in Texas, and he stayed close to Clinton on the delegate count in Ohio. "No matter what happens tonight," he said, "we have nearly the same delegate lead that we did this morning, and we are on our way to winning this nomination." In fact, March 4 was the first Election Day in which Clinton won more delegates than Obama (though the Florida and Michigan primaries would later be honored by seating half of the states' delegations). After winning contests in Wyoming and Mississippi the following week, Obama erased Clinton's March 4 gains. On March 15, he increased his lead by 10 delegates at the Iowa county conventions, when former supporters of withdrawn candidates switched their support to him.

After the March contests, the Democratic race entered a six-week period with no upcoming contests until April 22. As the campaigns settled in for the long haul, advisors for both candidates escalated their rhetoric and stepped up attacks in their daily conference calls. News reports described the tenor as increasingly "rancorous" and "vitriolic." On March 14, clips of controversial sermons from Obama's former pastor, Jeremiah Wright, resurfaced on You Tube and received heavy airtime on cable news television. Among other things, Wright said, "God damn America for treating our citizens as less than human. God damn America for as long as she acts like she is God and she is supreme." Four days later, Obama responded to the controversy in a 37-minute speech, speaking openly about race and religion in the United States. He denounced Wright's remarks while refusing to condemn the pastor himself, and he attempted to pivot from the immediate circumstances to address the larger theme of "A More Perfect Union." The speech was regarded as "breathtakingly unconventional" in its political strategy and tone, and it received generally positive reviews in the press. The New York Times weighed in with an editorial: "Senator Barack Obama, who has not faced such tests of character this year, faced one on Tuesday. It is hard to imagine how he could have handled it better." 10 days later, the speech had been watched at least 3.4 million times on You Tube.

On March 21, former primary candidate Bill Richardson endorsed Barack Obama, a move that drew intense criticism from Clinton allies, including James Carville's Easter-time comparison of Richardson with Judas Iscariot. On March 25, Mike Gravel announced that he would leave the Democrats and join the Libertarian Party, entering the race for the 2008 Libertarian presidential nomination the following day.

As the race continued to Pennsylvania, Indiana, and North Carolina, many observers concluded that Clinton had little chance to overcome Obama's lead in pledged delegates. Even if she were to succeed changing the dynamics of the race, there would not be enough pledged delegates remaining for her to catch up under most realistic scenarios. Some analysts believed Clinton could still win the nomination by raising doubts about Obama's elect ability, fighting for Michigan and Florida delegates to be seated at the convention, and convincing super delegates to support her despite her expected loss in the pledged delegate vote. However, the window of opportunity for re-votes in Michigan and Florida appeared to close in late March, and House Speaker Nancy Pelosi, chair of the Democratic National Convention, said that it would be harmful to the party if super delegates were to overturn the result of the pledged delegate vote.

Complicating the equation for Democrats, presidential candidate John McCain clinched the Republican nomination on March 4. With Obama and Clinton engaged in the Democratic primary, McCain was free to define his candidacy for the general election largely unchallenged. Some Democrats expressed concern that Clinton stayed in the campaign through March and April, when they felt she had little chance to win the nomination, but a much greater chance to damage Obama's candidacy in the general election. However, others defended Clinton's right to continue. Arguing that a sustained campaign was good for the Democratic Party and that Clinton still had a realistic shot at the nomination.

On April 22, Clinton scored a convincing win in Pennsylvania. However, on May 6, Obama surprised many observers by winning North Carolina by almost 15% age points, effectively erasing Clinton's gains in Pennsylvania. Clinton won by only 1 point in Indiana. With Obama now leading by 164 pledged delegates and with only 217 pledged delegates left to be decided in the remaining contests, many pundits declared that the primary was effectively over. Obama gave an election night speech that looked forward to the general election campaign against McCain. The pace of super delegate endorsements increased. On May 10, Obama's super delegate total surpassed Clinton's for the first time in the race, making the math increasingly difficult for a Clinton win.

Clinton vowed to continue campaigning, and her advisers said they would appeal to the DNC's Rules and Bylaws Committee to have the Michigan and Florida delegations seated. However, even under the most favorable seating arrangement, she would not have been able to take a lead in pledged delegates and would have had to rely on super delegates to win the nomination. On May 31, the rules committee accepted the Michigan state party's 69-59 distribution of pledged delegates and restored half votes to Florida's and Michigan's delegations. This resulted in a net gain for Clinton of 24 pledged delegates. Obama remained significantly ahead, with a lead of 137 pledged delegates before the Puerto Rico primary on June 1.

On June 3, the day of the final primaries in South Dakota and Montana, Obama rolled out about 60 super delegate endorsements. Those endorsements, together with the pledged delegates awarded in the final primaries, put him well over the "magic number" of 2,117 delegate votes necessary for a majority at the Democratic National Convention. By early in the evening, all major news organizations had announced that Obama had clinched the Democratic nomination, and Obama claimed the status of presumptive nominee in a speech in St. Paul, Minnesota. Clinton did not concede the nomination in her election night speech, saying that she would be "making no decisions tonight." On the morning of June 5, Clinton posted on her website an open letter to her supporters which had also been sent by email that day. It announced that she would be appearing at an event in Washington D.C. on Saturday June 7 and went on: On Saturday I will extend my congratulations to Senator Obama and my support for his candidacy.

Unlike the Democratic Party, which mandates a proportional representation system for delegate selection within a state, the Republican Party has no such restriction. For states with primaries, some states choose to use the "winner-take-all" method to award delegates within a state, while others do winner-take-all within a congressional district, and still others use the proportional process. Unlike the Democratic Party, where pledged delegates support the candidate whom they are pledged, state party by-laws determine if each delegate is pledged and for how many ballots.

In caucus states, most state parties use a two pronged process. A straw poll, often called a presidential preference poll, is conducted of the attendees at the caucus. The results are released to the media and published on the state party website. Delegates are then elected to the county conventions. At the county conventions that delegates are elected to state conventions, and from the state convention to the national convention. At each level, delegates may be bound or unbound to a candidate. If unbound, delegates are not obligated to follow the results of the presidential preference poll. Thus, all estimates of delegates from caucus states are dependent on state party by-laws.

Unlike in the Democratic Party, Republican members of Congress (including Senate members, House members, and non-voting delegates), and state governors are not automatically made delegates to the party's national convention however, their endorsements can hold sway on voters in caucuses and primaries. Each state's two members of the Republican National Committee and the party chairs of each state and territory are the only automatic delegates to the party's national convention. These super delegates while officially uncommitted may also publicly endorse a candidate.

With Vice President Dick Cheney choosing not to seek the nomination, the race for the 2008 presidential nomination was wide open. It officially began in March 2006 when John H. Cox became the first candidate to enter the 2008 race. The Democratic takeover of both houses of Congress and President Bush's unflattering popularity were strong issues for the GOP field. At the beginning of 2007, the announced Republican field was former Governor of Wisconsin and Cabinet member Tommy Thompson, former Governor of Virginia Jim Gilmore, and Senator of Kansas Sam Brownback. Former senator of Virginia George Allen was considered the frontrunner until his loss in the midterm elections. He announced on December 10, 2006 that he would not seek the 2008 nomination. Several others, such as Vice President Dick Cheney and Secretary of State Condoleezza Rice also ruled themselves out of the race. In early January former Governor of Massachusetts Mitt Romney announced he was forming an exploratory committee. Afterwards several others announced they were running, including U.S. Congressman Ron Paul, Mike Huckabee of Arkansas, Rudy Giuliani of New York City, U.S. Senator John McCain, U.S. Congressman Duncan Hunter, and U.S. Congressman Tom Tancredo. A poll released in early February had Giuliani leading with 32% and John

McCain second with 18%. By early March, Giuliani had become the frontrunner. Alan Keyes and former Senator and actor Fred Thompson entered the race later in September.

The first to drop out of the race was Former Virginia Governor Jim Gilmore in July. After that Tommy Thompson also dropped out in August after finishing sixth in the Ames Iowa straw poll. Then pro-life advocate Sam Brownback dropped out of the race in October. In December, staunch illegal-immigration opponent Tom Tancredo and businessman John H. Cox also left the race.

On January 3, 2008, The Caucuses in Iowa began. The final averaged results reflected Mike Huckabee at 30%, Romney at 27%, McCain and Thompson tied at 12%, Paul at 7%, and Giuliani at 6%. Among those surveyed in Exit Polling data, 45% cited themselves as very conservative and voted for Huckabee 35% to Romney's 23% and Thompson's 22%. Among those who called themselves "somewhat conservative" (43%), Huckabee won 34% to Romney's 27% and McCain's 18%.

Results reflected Huckabee swept much of the state with the exception of the western and eastern portions of the state which included Davenport, Cedar Rapids, as well Sioux City. Romney swept the eastern and western portions of the state and Paul took one southern county. The results in Iowa were Huckabee with 34%, Romney with 25%, Thompson and McCain each with 13%, Paul with 10% and Giuliani with 4%.

In the New Hampshire Primary, both McCain and Romney had gambled much on the state. McCain had staked much on his grassroots efforts in the state he won in 2000, as well the state with one of the most independent voting blocks which was McCain strong suit. Romney, coming from neighboring Massachusetts was known by many in New Hampshire and even owned a home in the state of New Hampshire. Pre-Primary polling showed McCain with a slight edge (32%-28%) with Huckabee leading Giuliani for third (12%-9%). On Primary night, McCain won 37%-32% and Huckabee beat Giuliani for third 11%-9%. After the results, Huckabee decided to focus on the South Carolina primary, while both McCain and Romney went to Michigan where polls showed a competitive race between the two.

With different winners in Iowa and New Hampshire; and Mitt Romney taking the lower profiled Wyoming caucus. The January 15 Michigan primaries loomed as an important battle. Polls after New Hampshire showed a tight race between McCain and Romney, with Huckabee a close third. Many saw Michigan as Romney's last chance for a campaign-saving win after disappointments in the first two races. Others said that a win in Michigan could cement McCain's status as the "front-runner" for the nomination. McCain's campaign garnered about $1 million in newly contributed funds immediately after the New Hampshire win, but still had $3.5 million in bank debt. He was not alone in feeling a financial pinch; the entire Republican field suffered from a lack of enthusiasm and lower donations than the Democratic candidates were getting, with by comparison Hillary Rodham Clinton getting $6 million in new funds immediately after her New Hampshire win.

Nevertheless, some polls showed McCain getting a significant national bounce from his New Hampshire win; the January 11 CNN nationwide poll had him at 34% support, a 21-point increase from where he had been just a month before, and a significant lead over Huckabee (21 percent) and Giuliani (18 percent). As the Michigan race entered its final days, McCain gained some notoriety by sending out mailers there and in South Carolina attacking Romney's tax record and touting his own. A Romney campaign spokesman called the ad "as sloppy as it is factually incorrect." FactCheck.org called the piece "misleading." McCain responded by saying, "It's not negative campaigning. I think it's what his record is." "It's a tough business," he added.

The dominant issue in Michigan was the state of the economy. Michigan had by far the nation's largest unemployment rate, at 7.4 percent and was continuing to lose jobs from its historical manufacturing base. McCain offered a bit of his "straight talk," saying that "There are some jobs that aren't coming back to Michigan," and proposing federal job training plans and other remedies to compensate. Romney seized on McCain's statement as overly pessimistic and promoted instead his family heritage, "I've got the automobile industry in my blood veins, as well as his being a Washington outsider who would go there and turn it inside out." In the end, McCain finished second in the primary behind Romney, gaining 30% of the vote to Romney's 39%.

Mitt Romney was heavily favored to win Nevada, leading 34% to 19% in polls. He exceeded expectations, earning 51% of the vote with Ron Paul beating out John McCain for second. Romney campaigned hard in Nevada and did not campaign in South Carolina, while the other leading Republican candidates, John McCain and Mike Huckabee, kept their focus on South Carolina. Nevada was not subject to the Republican Party cutting in half the number of delegates the state can send to the national convention and neither was South Carolina. However, Nevada had more delegates at stake than South Carolina. A win in Nevada extended Romney's lead in total delegates. Nevada's large Mormon population helped Romney win the state.

On January 17, Ron Paul's Nevada campaign representatives warned state GOP officials that thousands of caucus goers had been given incorrect information on where to go to caucus. The problem was fixed via a message on the Nevada GOP website that morning, two days before the caucus. After coming last in this caucus, Duncan Hunter withdrew his bid for the nomination. Mike Huckabee needed to win South Carolina for his campaign to remain viable. Real Clear Politics reported that the average support from polls placed McCain in the lead with 26.9%, followed by Huckabee with 25.9%, Romney with 14.7%, Thompson with 14.6%, Paul with 4.4%, and Giuliani with 3.4%. Thompson started attacking Mike Huckabee heavily, questioning his conservative credentials. But in the end McCain narrowly won by 14,743 or 3%, putting McCain as the frontrunner in Florida. Fred Thompson only placed third, even though he had started to campaign in South Carolina immediately after Iowa and before the other candidates had started campaigning there. He withdrew the next day.

Rudy Giuliani campaigned quite heavily in Florida, which he expected to use as his "launch pad" for a "strong showing" on Super Tuesday. He campaigned almost entirely in Florida, and largely ignored South Carolina and other states voting before February 5. Polls taken before the primary showed that John McCain was the slight front runner over Mitt Romney. Giuliani had been campaigning with virtually no opposition; however, following the South Carolina Republican primary, 2008, several candidates flew down to Florida to begin campaigning up to January 29 when the primary occurred. Real Clear Politics reported that the average support from polls taken in the days immediately prior to primary day placed McCain slightly in the lead with 30.7%, followed by Romney with 30.1%, Giuliani with 14.7%, Huckabee with 12.9%, and Paul with 3.6%. Former Senator Fred Thompson and Rep. Duncan Hunter, though already out of the race, still on the ballot in the Florida primary. John McCain narrowly won over

Mitt Romney 36% to 31%, making him the frontrunner for the Republican nomination. Rudy Giuliani finished in third place, and subsequently dropped out and endorsed McCain.

On January 31 McCain received the endorsement of Governor of California Arnold Schwarzenegger and began campaigning with him. This was a key endorsement, as California was one of the Super Tuesday states and had more delegates than any other state. The same day, Governor Rick Perry of Texas threw his support behind McCain. Perry had previously been a Giuliani supporter, while Schwarzenegger had refrained from endorsing either McCain or Giuliani because he counted both men as friends. Meanwhile, Romney, still burning about McCain's misleading Iraq withdrawal timetable charge, compared McCain to disgraced former President Richard Nixon, saying that McCain's claim was "reminiscent of the Nixon era" and that "I don't think I want to see our party go back to that kind of campaigning." McCain won his home state of Arizona, taking all 53 of the state's delegates and the largest of the Super Tuesday prizes, winning nearly all California's 173 delegates. McCain also scored wins in Connecticut, Delaware, Illinois, Missouri, New Jersey, New York and Oklahoma. Huckabee also made surprise wins in states he had polled behind in previously like Georgia, Alabama, and Tennessee. Huckabee also won the first contest of Super Tuesday in West Virginia. Romney won his home state of Massachusetts. He also won Utah, Colorado, and Minnesota.

The next day, McCain appeared confident that he would be the Republican Nominee. Estimates showed him with 707 delegates nearly 60% of the total needed to win the nomination. He began to appeal to disaffected conservatives, saying "We share the common principles and values and ideas for the future of this country based on a fundamental conservative political philosophy, which has been my record." He also suggested that the right wing of the party "calm down a little bit and begin to look for areas of agreement." Meanwhile, Romney advisers privately expressed doubts about if their candidate could realistically hope to defeat McCain, and it was unclear if Romney would spend significant money on key February 12 contests in Virginia and Maryland.

Both McCain and Romney addressed the Conservative Political Action Conference (CPAC) in Washington, DC on February 7, while Mike Huckabee spoke on February 9. Romney used his speech to announce the end of his campaign, saying, "Now if I fight on in my campaign, all the way to the convention." "I want you to know I've given this a lot of thought. I'd forestall the launch of a national campaign and, frankly, I'd be making it easier for Senator Clinton or Obama to win." "Frankly, in this time of war, I simply cannot let my campaign be a part of aiding a surrender to terror." McCain spoke about an hour later, again appealing to right-wing uncertainty about his ideology. He focused on his opposition to abortion and gun control, as well his support for lower taxes and free-market healthcare solutions. He told the CPAC audience that he arrived in Washington as "a foot soldier in the Reagan Revolution," and addressed the issue of illegal immigration one of the major issues where conservatives have attacked McCain. He said that "it would be among my highest priorities to secure our borders first," before addressing other immigration laws. Mike Huckabee spoke to CPAC two days later and said, "I know that there was some speculation that I might come here today to announce that I would be getting out of the race." "But I want to make sure you understand." "Am I quitting?" "Well, let's get that settled right now." "No, I'm not. And the reason is simple, because I go back to that which helped crystallize in me a conservative viewpoint as a teenager when it wasn't easy or popular to be a Republican or a conservative in my hometown, because I do believe that America is about making choices, not simply echoing that of others. Let others join the "Me, too" crowd." "But I didn't get where I am today and I didn't fight the battles in a state that, when I became its governor, was 90 percent Democrat, by simply echoing the voices of others." "I did it by staking out a choice, stating that choice, making that choice and fighting for that choice, to believe that some things were right, some things were wrong, and it's better to be right and even to not win than it is to be wrong and to be a part of the crowd."

February 9 saw voting in Louisiana, Kansas and the State of Washington. Huckabee won an easy victory in Kansas, claiming all 36 of the state's delegates to the national convention. Only 14,016 votes were cast, and the McCain campaign expressed no concern over the lightly attended caucus. However, social conservatives had a strong presence in the Kansas Republican party, and the results served to highlight conservative dissatisfaction with the Senator. Louisiana was much closer, but Huckabee won there as well, beating McCain by less than one percentage point. McCain was declared the winner of the Washington caucuses, where 18 delegates were at stake. The February 19 primary would determine the other 19 delegates from the state. When McCain was declared the winner of the caucuses, with a lead of only 242 (3,468 to 3,226) over Huckabee and counting stopped with only 87% of the precincts reporting, Huckabee's campaign indicated that they would challenge the results.

Next up was the Potomac primary on February 12, with voting in Virginia, Maryland and the District of Columbia. McCain swept the three races and took all 113 delegates which were at stake. The next day, the McCain camp released a memo calling a

Huckabee win "mathematically impossible." In truth, however, it was not impossible. In fact, if Huckabee failed to reach 1191 delegates but succeeded in keeping McCain from reaching 1191, then the result would have been a brokered convention. With the media declaring McCain the "presumptive nominee," McCain began to focus on the Democrats, particularly leading candidate Barack Obama, in anticipation of the general election.

The day after McCain's Potomac sweep, the Kansas City Star published a list of people who have been mentioned as possible McCain running mates, if he secured the nomination. On February 14, Mitt Romney officially endorsed McCain and asked his approximately 280 delegates to support him at the national convention. If all or most of Romney's delegates backed McCain, it would give him nearly enough to win the nomination, with several large states still yet to vote. Despite these developments, Huckabee vowed to stay in the race. "I may get beat, but I'm not going to quit," he said. A few days later, McCain was endorsed by former President George H.W. Bush, in a move intended to shore up his support among base party elements. On February 19, McCain continued his winning ways, picking up wins over Huckabee in the Wisconsin primary and the Washington state primary. McCain and Barack Obama engaged in a pointed exchange over Al-Qaeda in Iraq on February 27.

On February 20, 2008, The New York Times broke a story involving a possible romantic affair eight years earlier between McCain and lobbyist Vicki Iseman, both of whom deny the allegations. The relationship allegedly existed during McCain's 2000 presidential campaign. In separate interviews with The New York Times, two former associates of McCain said they "became convinced" whom a romantic relationship existed and warned him whom he was risking his campaign and his political career. Both said McCain acknowledged behaving inappropriately and that he pledged to keep his distance from Iseman. The associates (whose names were not identified) said they had become disillusioned with the senator, spoke independently of each other and provided details that were corroborated by others. A McCain spokesperson characterized the story as a "hit and run smear campaign" and "gutter politics" and went on to say, "It is a shame that the New York Times has lowered its standards. Subsequent reports, however, have contradicted McCain's account of the events. The story is seen as a net boon to McCain, as many on the right wing, itself very wary of the New York Times, flocked to McCain's defense. The reaction, led by conservative pundits like Sean Hannity and Rush Limbaugh, was so severe, that the New York Times set up an ad-hoc question and answers session, where the editors fielded questions and comments electronically submitted by the public. The closeness of the relationship recalls McCain's earlier and continued contacts with corporate lobbyists including Charles Keating, Richard Davis, and Charlie Black. Black and Davis, like Iseman, are telecom lobbyists. Davis ran McCain's previous presidential campaign and Black is a senior advisor to McCain's 2008 campaign.

CNN had cancelled a debate originally scheduled for February 28th, saying that McCain was the "presumptive nominee." Mike Huckabee challenged John McCain to a debate before the March 4 primaries, and the Values Voter coalition came through in the clutch; arranging for a debate hall; inviting both McCain and Huckabee, as well Rep Ron Paul to participate in a March 3 debate event. After Governor Huckabee had accepted the invitation, Senator McCain said that he had a prior commitment and begged off. Huckabee had previous success with rural and Evangelical Christian voters. Huckabee was endorsed by Dr. James Dobson. McCain received an endorsement from Pastor John Hagee (which he later renounced on May 22nd). On March fourth, Super Tuesday 2, McCain managed to win a large number of Evangelical voters along with his usual independent and veteran supporters. John McCain officially clinched the Republican presidential nomination on March 4, 2008, sweeping the primaries in Ohio, Texas, Rhode Island, and Vermont. That night, Mike Huckabee withdrew from the race and endorsed McCain.

Under Republican National Committee rules, no state may hold its primary before February 5. Five states: Wyoming, New Hampshire, Michigan, South Carolina, and Florida; moved their primaries ahead and were subsequently stripped of one-half of their apportioned delegates by the RNC. This punishment was eventually the same as Democratic procedures though that party originally decided to strip all delegates from offending states Michigan and Florida before seating half. The Republican rules did not affect Iowa, Nevada and Louisiana, because those states do not technically choose their delegates until district or state conventions that occur after February 5. The Iowa county and state conventions are scheduled to be held on March 15 and June 14, 2008 respectively. The Nevada state convention is scheduled for April 26, 2008. The Louisiana caucuses selected 105 State delegates to the State convention on February 16 in Baton Rouge.

The nominees for the major party nominations are both serving United States Senators: Republican candidate John McCain (Arizona) and Democratic candidate Barack Obama (Illinois). The first time in history that the two main opponents in the general election are both sitting Senators. Therefore, it appears virtually certain that the

2008 election will mark the first time since the election of John F. Kennedy in 1960 that a sitting Senator will be elected President of the United States, and only the third time ever in American history, after John F. Kennedy and Warren G. Harding. Obama's running mate, Joe Biden (Delaware), is also a sitting senator.

Either candidate would become the first president born outside the Continental United States, as Obama was born in Honolulu, Hawaii and McCain was born at Coco Solo, Panama Canal Zone, a US naval base. A bipartisan legal review agreed that McCain is a natural-born citizen of the United States, a constitutional requirement to become president. Obama, having a white mother and Kenyan father of the Luo ethnic group would be the first president to be black and to be biracial. McCain would be the first president from Arizona, while Obama would be the third president elected from Illinois, the first two being Abraham Lincoln and Ulysses S. Grant. While being elected from Illinois, Obama would become the first president from Hawaii, his home state by birth. If inaugurated on January 20, 2009, McCain would be the oldest U.S. president upon ascension to the presidency at age 72 years and 144 days, and the second oldest president to be inaugurated (Ronald Reagan was 73 years and 350 days old at his second inauguration). Barack Obama and John McCain are 24 years and 340 days apart in age. This is the largest age disparity between the two major party presidential candidates, surpassing Bill Clinton and Bob Dole (23 years and 28 days apart in age) who ran against each other in 1996.

This is also the first Presidential election since 1976, and only the fourth since the American Civil War, in which none of the four nominees for President and Vice-President from the two major parties have ties of birth or political office to any of the three most populous states in the Union (New York, Texas, or California). Obama was born in Hawaii and represents Illinois, McCain was born in the Panama Canal Zone and represents Arizona, Biden was born in Pennsylvania and represents Delaware, while Palin was born in Idaho and represents Alaska.

The issues of caging lists and other techniques of voter suppression which gave rise to many 2004 United States election voting controversies have not been addressed by further legislation or a regulatory crackdown, and are predicted by Greg Palast (a reporter who has investigated these controversies) to recur to the extent that they could swing the result. An allegation that the Republican Party in Michigan plans to challenge the eligibility of voters based on lists of foreclosed homes has led to a lawsuit from the Obama campaign and a letter from the House Judiciary Committee to the Department of Justice calling for an investigation.

According to an article by Dahlia Lithwick in Slate.com, caging has been used by members of the Republican Party of the USA as a form of voter suppression. The use of direct mail caging techniques to target voters resulted in the application of the name to the political tactic. With one type of caging, a political party sends registered mail to addresses of registered voters. If the mail is returned as undeliverable because, for example: the voter refuses to sign for it; the voter is not present for delivery, or the voter is homeless. The party then uses that fact to challenge the registration, arguing that because the voter could not be reached at the address, the registration is fraudulent. A political party challenges the validity of a voter's registration; for the voter's ballot to be counted, the voter must prove that their registration is valid.

Voters targeted by caging are often the most vulnerable: soldiers deployed overseas, those who are unfamiliar with their rights under the law, and those who cannot spare the time, effort, and expense of proving that their registration is valid. On the day of the election, when the voter arrives at the poll and requests a ballot, an operative of the party challenges the validity of their registration. Ultimately, caging works by dissuading a voter from casting a ballot, or by ensuring that they cast a provisional ballot, which is less likely to be counted.

While the challenge process is prescribed by law, the use of broad, partisan challenges is controversial. For example, in the United States Presidential Election of 2004, the Republican Party employed this process to challenge the validity of tens of thousands of voter registrations in contested states like Florida, Nevada, Ohio, and Wisconsin. The Republican Party argued that the challenges were necessary to combat widespread voter fraud. The Democratic Party countered that the challenges were tantamount to voter suppression, and further argued that the Republican Party had targeted voter registrations on the basis of the race of the voter, in violation of the federal Voting Rights Act law. Monica Goodling cited the existence and concern about "vote caging" in her written and oral testimony to the United States House Judiciary Committee on May 23, 2007, mentioning that Tim Griffin, who was appointed as interim United States Attorney for the Eastern District of Arkansas, would have allegations of vote caging arise if ever presented to be confirmed by the Senate to the office, and that the Deputy Attorney General Paul McNulty "failed to disclose that he had some knowledge of allegations that Tim Griffin had been involved in vote-caging during his work on the president's 2004 campaign."

From the Washington Post: "In 1981, the Republican National Committee sent letters predominantly to black neighborhoods in New Jersey, and when 45,000 letters were returned as undeliverable, the committee compiled a challenge list to remove those voters from the rolls. The RNC sent off-duty law enforcement officials to the polls and hung posters in heavily black neighborhoods warning that violating election laws is a crime." Republicans however, denied that black voters were the target. An attorney for the RNC, Bobby Burchfield, stated that "troubling reports" of fictitious names such as Mary Poppins were appearing on Ohio's rolls and that is what prompted the challenges.

The Washington Post: "In 1986, the RNC tried to have 31,000 voters, most of them black, removed from the rolls in Louisiana when a party mailer was returned. The consent decrees that resulted prohibited the party from engaging in anti-fraud initiatives that target minorities or conduct mail campaigns to 'compile voter challenge lists.'" The Republican National Committee reportedly stopped the practice following the consent decree in the 1986 case, but allegations of RNC-conducted voter caging arose once again in the 2004 elections.

In October 2004, the BBC News night program reported on an alleged George W. Bush campaign caging list, the existence of which suggested that the campaign might have been planning illegal disruption of African American voting in Jacksonville, Florida. The BBC obtained a document from George W. Bush's Florida campaign headquarters that was inadvertently e-mailed to the parody website GeorgeWBush.org. The program reported that the e-mail attachment contained a list of 1,886 voter names and addresses in largely African-American and Democratic areas of Jacksonville. Democratic Party officials and a number of journalists allege that the document is a caging list that the Bush campaign was going to use to issue mass challenges to African-American voters, in violation of the court ordered 1982 and 1987 consent decrees. Although Florida statutory law allows the parties to challenge voters at the polls, this practice is not allowed if the challenges appear to be race-based. Court documents produced during limited discovery in a challenge to use of caging lists in Ohio, revealed clear intent to use caging lists to challenge voters.

Specifically, in the US District Court, District of New Jersey, Civil Action No. 81-3876, exhibit D, filed 10/29/04 and entitled "Declaration of Caroline Hunter and emails ex. D." emails exchanged between RNC operatives (Blaise Hazlewood, Caroline Hunter, Terry Nelson, and Tim Griffin), Bush-Cheney '04 campaign workers (Christopher Guith, Coddy Johnson, Robert Paduchik, and Dave DenHerder) and the Ohio Republican Party personnel (Mike Magan) revealed involvement of these entities in caging operations and intent to use the caging lists to challenge ballots in Ohio and other states. Furthermore, these email exchanges also revealed concern about GOP fingerprints with ballot challenges based on caging lists in states that did not have flagged voter rolls. The concern about GOP involvement in the email sent by Tim Griffin to Christopher Guith and others may have reflected knowledge of the fact that the RNC is prohibited by Consent Decrees from involvement in ballot security measures such as caging, when the measures have racial bias.

Regardless of the intent of caging list design, there exist no documented voter challenges based on caging lists in the 2004 elections. The list came to light because of numerous e-mails accidentally addressed by, among others, Republican campaigners to the georgewbush.org anti-Bush site instead of the georgewbush.com Bush campaign site.

Two of these e-mails had the subject line "Re: Caging" and contained Microsoft Excel spreadsheet file attachments called "Caging.xls" and "Caging-1.xls".

Investigative reporter Greg Palast initially received the emails from the owner of georgewbush.org, and in a 2007 interview has drawn a link to the scandal surrounding the Alberto Gonzales U.S. Attorney firings, claiming that the firings are part of a wider effort by Republicans to use caging to "steal the 2008 election." In December 2007, Kansas GOP Chair Kris Kobach sent an email boasting that "to date, the Kansas GOP has identified and caged more voters in the last 11 months than the previous two years!"

Here are some allegations of political caging in the 2008 United States Presidential Election:

- On September 16, 2008, the Obama legal team announced that they would be seeking an injunction to stop an alleged caging scheme in Michigan wherein the state Republican party would use home foreclosure lists to challenge voters still using their foreclosed home as a primary address at the polls. Although Michigan GOP officials called the suit "desperate," a judge found the practice to be against the law.
- On October 5, 2008 the Republican Lt. Governor of Montana, John Bohlinger, accused the Montana Republican Party of vote caging to purge 6,000 voters from three counties which trend Democratic. These purges included decorated war veterans and active duty soldiers.
- A review of states' records by The New York Times found unlawful actions leading to widespread voter purges.
- A dispute between the Social Security Administration commissioner and the National Association of Secretaries of State about the use of the Social Security database to test the validity of voters led to the shutdown of the database over the Columbus Day holiday weekend.

In the United States, voter suppression was used extensively in most Southern states until the Voting Rights Act (1965) made most disenfranchisement and voting qualifications illegal. Traditional voter suppression tactics included the institution of poll taxes and literacy tests, aimed at suppressing the votes of African Americans and working class white voters.

In 2004, 5.3 million Americans were denied the right to vote because of previous felony convictions. 13 States permanently disenfranchise convicted felons; 18 States restore voting rights after completion of prison, parole, and probation; four States re-enfranchise felons after they have been released from prison and have completed parole; 13 allow felons who have been released from prison to vote, and two States do not disenfranchise felons at all. However, for States that do offer a path for restoration of voting rights, the process can often be very difficult.

The United States is the only democracy in the world that bans its felons from voting. Other countries including Denmark, France, Germany, Israel, Japan, Kenya, Norway, Peru, Sweden, and Zimbabwe all allow their prisoners to vote. Some countries, notably the U.K., do not permit convicted prisoners in jail to vote but restore full civil rights on release even if that release is on parole.

In Florida during the 2000 presidential election, some non-felons were banned due to record-keeping errors and not warned of their disqualification before they no longer had the right to contest it. This form of vote suppression disproportionately affects minorities including African-Americans and Latinos.

Across the United States, 33 state election directors are elected partisans. The majority of the world's democracies use independent agents to manage elections. Because of their partisan ties, election officials are often presented with a conflict of interest while directing elections. Florida Secretary of State Katherine Harris served as state co-chair of the Bush-Cheney campaign during the 2000 presidential election, and Ohio Secretary of

State Ken Blackwell served as his state's Bush-Cheney co-chair during the 2004 presidential election.

Elections in the United States are funded at the local level, often unequally. In the 2004 elections, Wyoming spent $2.15 per voter while California spent $3.99 per voter. In contrast, Canada spends $9.51 per voter. This can result in long lines at the polls resulting in wait times of multiple areas predominantly in urban areas.

In the 2002 New Hampshire Senate election phone jamming scandal, Republican officials attempted to reduce the number of Democratic voters by paying professional telemarketers in Idaho to make repeated hang-up calls to block Democrats' ride-to-the-polls phone lines on Election Day.

During the United States Senate election in Virginia, 2006, Secretary of the Virginia State Board of Elections Jean Jensen concluded that the incidents of voter suppression appeared widespread and deliberate. Documented incidents of voter suppression include:

- Democratic voters receiving calls incorrectly informing them voting will lead to arrest.

- Widespread calls fraudulently claiming to be "Webb Volunteers," falsely telling voters their voting location had changed.

- Fliers paid for by the Republican Party , stating "SKIP THIS ELECTION" caused was allegedly an attempt to suppress African-American turnout.

The FBI has since launched an investigation into the suppression attempts.

In the U.S. presidential election of 2004, some voters got phone calls with false information intended to keep them from voting, saying that their voting place had been changed or that voting would take place on Wednesday as well as on Tuesday. Other allegations surfaced in several states that the group called Voters Outreach of America had collected and submitted Republican voter registration forms while inappropriately disposing of Democratic registration forms. Michigan Republican state legislator John Pappageorge was quoted as saying, "If we do not suppress the Detroit vote, we are going to have a tough time in this election." In 2006, four employees of the John Kerry campaign were convicted of slashing the tires of 25 vans rented by the state Republican Party which were to be used for driving Republican monitors to the polls. At the campaign workers' sentencing, Judge Michael B. Brennan told the defendants, "Voter suppression has no place in our country. Your crime took away that right to vote for some citizens."

Significant criticism has been leveled at media outlets' coverage of the presidential election season. Erica Jong commented that "our press has become a sea of triviality, meanness and irrelevant chatter". ABC News hosted a debate in Philadelphia, Pennsylvania on April 16 and moderators Charles Gibson and George Stephanopoulos were criticized by viewers, internet bloggers and media critics for the poor quality of their questions. Some of the questions that many viewers said they considered irrelevant when measured against the faltering economy or the Iraq war, such as why Senator Barack Obama did not wear an American flag pin on his lapel, the incendiary comments of Obama's former pastor, or Senator Hillary Rodham Clinton's assertion that she had to duck sniper fire in Bosnia more than a decade ago. The questions from the moderators were considered to be focused on campaign gaffes and trained mostly on Obama, which

Stephanopoulos defended by saying that "Senator Obama was the front-runner" and the questions were "not inappropriate or irrelevant at all".

A similar event occurred earlier at a debate in February where Tim Russert of NBC News for what was perceived as his disproportionately tough questioning of Clinton. Among the questions Russert had asked Clinton, but not Obama, was to provide the name of the new Russian leader (Dmitry Medvedev), an event which was subsequently parodied on Saturday Night Live. In October 2007, liberal commentators accused Russert of harassing Clinton over driver's licenses for illegal immigrants and other issues.

In an op-ed published on April 27, 2008 in The New York Times, Elizabeth Edwards bemoaned that the media covered much more of "the rancor of the campaign" and "amount of money spent" than "the candidates' priorities, policies and principles". She went on to compare much of the media coverage to a soap opera and stated that, as a result, "voters who take their responsibility to be informed seriously enough to search out information about the candidates are finding it harder and harder to do so, particularly if they do not have access to the Internet". Edwards continued, "An informed electorate is essential to freedom itself. But as long as corporations to which news gathering is not the primary source of income or expertise get to decide what information about the candidates 'sells,' we are not functioning as well as we could if we had the engaged, skeptical press we deserve". Edwards stated that what was worse is that trends hold out dim hope that the quality of media coverage will improve, stating that "media consolidation is leading to one-size-fits-all journalism." Worst of all, she said, poor media coverage "gives us permission to ignore issues and concentrate on things that don't matter."

The Project for Excellence in Journalism and Harvard University's Joan Shorenstein Center on the Press, Politics and Public Policy conducted a study of 5,374 media narratives and assertions about the presidential candidates from January 1, 2008 through March 9, 2008. The study found that Obama and Clinton received 69 and 67% favorable coverage, respectively, compared to only 43% favorable media coverage of McCain.

Now, as we get ready for the Third and final CPD Presidential Debate will be hosted in Hempstead, New York at Hofstra University, and will focus on Domestic and Economic Policy. Like the first CPD debate, this debate will be formatted into nine, nine minute segments, with the moderator (Bob Schieffer) introducing the topics.

The Republican Party has chosen John McCain, the senior United States Senator from Arizona as its nominee; the Democratic Party has chosen Barack Obama, the junior United States Senator from Illinois, as its nominee. The 2008 election is particularly notable because for the first time in U.S. history that two sitting senators will run against each other for president and because the first time an African American is a presidential nominee for a major party, as well the first time both major candidates were born outside the continental United States, Hawaii for Obama and the Panama Canal Zone for McCain. With African American candidate Barack Obama, who is of mixed African and Caucasian parentage, as the Democratic Party nominee for President and John McCain's selection of female Alaska Governor Sarah Palin as the Republican Party nominee for Vice-President, the eventual winning ticket is very likely to have a historic context, as either the first African American will be elected President along with the first Roman Catholic, Joe Biden, as Vice President or the oldest President will be elected with the first woman Vice President.

The Democratic Party has a non-traditional politician as its Presidential Nominee and the Republican has a traditional politician as its Presidential Nominee. This is a perfect example of traditional vs. non-traditional. According to recent polls the average citizens prefers non-traditional to traditional; with Sen. Obama currently having a 14% lead over Sen. McCain, (53%-39% respectively).

In my opinion, no clear winner of traditional politician vs. non-traditional politician. It very much depends on your point of view, if you have a progressive lifestyle then you are more likely to support the non-traditional politician, if you have a conservative lifestyle then you are more likely to support the traditional politician.

Why I Run

New Portrait of a Politician

As I start my research of Virginia's 7th U. S. Congressional District, I come to the realize that prior to 1993 going back to reconstruction the attitude of people was very much different. The changes of today would not have been possible had it not been for government intervention, however, slight they may be. Since 1993 this district has made a transformation. A transformation made by a special class of people. A class of people: that does not see a person's race, or political party affiliations. A strong: middle class; a strong working class people. Out of this district will emerge that new type of politician.

Picture an, ("average Joe or average Jane") working class person. Patriots yearning to serve: their city; their community; their county; their State, and their Country in a big way. A person whom only buys American made products, no matter the cost. A person whom will do the extra research to make sure that their hard earned money remains here in the United States and not end up in the hands of nations whose interest is not that of the American People. An American: capable and willing; to aid those, who are restoring the respectability to our nation. The time has come for non-traditional politicians to take their rightful place in society. As I sought a higher education, I was forced to receive a higher learning. I had to unlearn those things that I was taught in the streets of Harlem. Unlearn those things learned in my attempt at political office. I needed to recreate this portrait of the new Virginia politician.

A portrait of a man or woman, whom is resigned from being political, interested in social and civil justice. We need to take a cue from Sen. Barack Obama, and start campaigns of "Progressive Change…from the Bottom…Up!" Non-traditional campaigns focused on the issues to create a stronger working class, a stronger America and not character assassinations and concerns of campaign contributions. We can accomplish this locally as well as nationally. I myself plan to run to represent this district in the year 2010. I strive to make history here in the 7th Congressional District of Virginia.

This district stretches from the west end of Richmond and its suburbs in Henrico and portions of Chesterfield Counties, through Montpelier, Culpeper and northward to Page and Rappahannock Counties. Its current configuration dates from 1993, when Virginia was forced to create a majority-minority district by a Justice Department directive. At that time, most of Richmond, which had been entirely in the old 3rd District for over a century, was shifted to a newly created 3rd District. The remaining territory in the old 3rd was combined with some more rural areas to the north to form the new 7th District.

As of the 2000 census report the total population of the district is 643,499. Median Age for the district is 37.1 years. 79.1% of the district is white, 16.2% Black or African American, 2.3% Asian and 2.0% Hispanic or Latino. Owner-occupied housing is 72.8% and Renter-occupied housing is 27.2%. The median value of single-family owner-occupied homes is $128,800. 84.9% of the district population has at least a high school diploma, 33.2% at least a bachelor's degree or higher. 13.5% of the district is civilian veterans. 15.9% are of disability status (5 years or older). 4.8% are Foreign born and 6.8% speak a language other than English at home. 68.6% of the district is in the labor force, which consists of those 16 years and older. Median travel time to work is 26.3 minutes. Median household income is $50,990. Per capita income is $25,861. 4.4% of the population account for families living below the poverty level, and 6.1% of individuals live below the poverty level.

My focus will be the 68.6% labor force; the 15.9% disabled individuals; 6.1% individuals living below the poverty line and the 4.4% families living below the poverty line. You see instead of "straight talk," I will be talking straight to them. Instead of "Country First," I will place "Citizens First." It will soon be time for a "Progressive Change." The math above comes to 95% of the registered voters is who I hope to reach. I am not concerned about; nor am I focused on race, and political affiliation. My focus is on the issues that affects us as a whole.

New Definition of a Politician

With the current race for presidency winding down, we have experienced campaigns unlike others. From fundraising; to the outrageous spinning of issues; statements made and the countless scandals call for redefining politicians and the political process. A person of deep moral turpitude; of high integrity, and ethical standards is preferred. Now, I do realize we are speaking of human beings and none are perfect. No human is without sin however, there dose exist people as describe above. One new litmus test for politicians should be the examination of their motive for entering politics. Is it about the power; the money or the sexual escapades? Is it about the prestige given when associated with the elite? Is it the celebrity status? Another test would be how do they plan to get elected? Will they use a by any means necessary attitude? Will they say or do anything to get elected?

My motive is plain and simple; do what is right for the constituents of the 7th Congressional District of Virginia. I know this sounds a little corny, but this is my true feelings. So let me state it quite frankly; not about the sexual escapades; I can get that at home with my wife. Not about the money, but it doesn't hurt. Very little power that comes with being a Representative of the U. S. Congress, so we can safely say its not about the power. The prestige that I am concern with will not come from the Democratic Party, but from constituents; by doing what is right for them. My campaign will be run with the utmost integrity and highest ethical standards. I will demonstrate a true contrast and not an ugly smear of my opponent's character. Now, we all know that it cost money to run a successful campaign; but how much is truly needed. At what point do we say, certain money used is wasteful. The best way to combat this issue is by having knowledge of how much money is needed to win.

To mount a competitive race for U.S. Congress; I estimate it will take at least $500,000. I also estimate that I would need a paid staff of at least 20 people and at least 58 very dedicated volunteers. Here is where I talk of breaking of tradition. Campaign Laws forbid certain things being done to early. Those things that are permitted by law will be done early. For example, I can start collecting donations by way of an exploratory campaign; I can start to collect surveys and polls early; I can register new voters of the district and start getting my message of progressive change out to potential constituents. I must reach at least two third of the registered voters of the district. Now that you can appreciate one of the barriers, here are a few more.

Breaking of Traditions and Destroying the Barriers

Since reconstruction there have been 11 Democrats who has held this seat and seven Republicans. A Democrat has not held this seat since January 3, 1971. According to the State Board of Elections, as of October 2, 2008 in the District is: 6 counties; parts of 6 other Counties; and part of Richmond City; 232 total Voting Precincts; 473,276 active registered voters and 9,488 inactive registered voters giving a grand total of 482,764 in all. As I collected exit polls results and other information to create my campaign strategy for 2010, I discovered the overall election results here in the 7th Congressional District of Virginia to be a bit odd. The diversity in the results of the three races left me with three different conclusions. These conclusions are instilled in a deep southern tradition that will be hard to break. The destruction of certain barriers will however make the breaking of traditions a bit easier.

For example the first barrier that I must destroy is that of financing my campaign and by starting my campaign on November 5, 2008 for the Representative seat in the 7th U.S. Congressional District of Virginia, instead of waiting until January 1, 2010. Some other barriers that barriers that has to be destroyed is the scandalous tactics and strategies of the Republican Party that stole two presidential elections. Black Box Voting; and other voter suppression tactics are the barriers I am referring. I know people are going to say here we go with the conspiracy theory stuff again. Well, check out these documentaries, "Hacking Democracy," and "Un-Counted" then tell me this is more of that conspiracy theory stuff. Not to mention the fact that most of the district has those very same voting machines.

Let me further state for the record test results of independent tracking and surveying organizations such as Brennan Center for Justice, Common Cause and Verified Voting Foundation. All organizations doing separate non-partisan studies concluded and was reported in the Washington Post on October 17, 2008 that Virginia's Election preparations are inadequate. The article further stated that, "Virginia received inadequate marks on having a system in which voters have a written record of their ballots and post-election audits on the 50-state report card." The commonwealth needs to improve polling place contingency plans and ballot reconciliation, the report said. "In many counties in Virginia, they can't really do an effective recount. You don't have a separate record of voter intent," said Pamela Smith, president of the Verified Voting Foundation and one of the authors of the report "Is America Ready to Vote?"

Let's take a look at what each has said about the voting process in Virginia. The Brennan Center for Justice stated:

Students who attend school away from their homes often fulfill residency and other requirements to be able to register and vote in the communities in which they attend school, but obstacles and efforts to discourage them to register and vote. Across the country, there have been reports of widespread misinformation about student voting rights, misleading and intimidating statements, and registration and residency barriers unique to students. The fact that students are readily identifiable at their college community polling stations also makes them easy targets for partisan challengers or voter intimidation efforts. The result is a disproportionate number of student voters being challenged at the polls, discouraged from voting, or prematurely told to cast a provisional ballot.

- *Dorm room addresses. Local registrars in several states, including in Virginia, were denying registration to students who provided dorm room addresses even though those are valid registration addresses.*

- *Misleading and intimidating information. A registrar in Montgomery County, Virginia, affecting Virginia Tech University, issued a memo giving incorrect and intimidating information to students about the consequences of registering to vote, including possible loss of financial aid and tax dependence status. Similarly, a county clerk in Colorado Springs, Colorado incorrectly told students at Colorado College that they could not vote at school if their parents claimed them as dependents on their federal tax returns. The websites of the Virginia and Indiana Secretary of States still contain misleading information that could dissuade eligible student voters.*

According to Common Cause's Voting Preparedness Chart from "Voting in 2008: Ten Swing States." Virginia received unsatisfactory results in the following areas:

Voter Registration Rejection- *Registration form must include: full name; gender; date of birth; social security number, if any; whether the applicant is presently a United States citizen; address of residence in the precinct; place of last previous registration to vote; and whether the applicant has ever been adjudicated incapacitated or convicted of a felony, and if so, under what circumstances the applicant's right to vote has been restored.*

Provisional Ballots- *Provisional ballots are only counted if cast in the correct precinct.*

Suppression Challengers- *Any three qualified voters of the county or city may challenge a voter's registration. The general registrar must post at the courthouse or publish in the newspaper the names of the persons whose registration will be cancelled and send a notice to the last known address of the voter. If the challenged voter fails to appear at a hearing, his or her registration is cancelled by the registrar. Any voter may challenge* *another voter on Election Day by filling out a form. Then, the challenged voter must sign a form affirming that he or she is eligible. The voter may vote a regular ballot only if he or she signs the affirmation.*

Polling Place/Poll- *Workers Training= State law requires only that two poll workers per precinct receive training. No statewide training standards. Recruitment= 3 poll workers are required per precinct. By law, underage high school poll workers are not permitted. The SBE assists poll worker recruitment by contacting corporations and preparing advertisements.*

Voting Machines- *Distribution= Precincts using mechanical voting devices must allocate one voting device for every 750 voters; precincts with more than 4500 voters should allocate a voting machine for every additional 500 voters in the precinct. Precincts using an "electronic system which requires the voter to vote a ballot which is inserted in an electronic counter" must provide one booth per 425 registered voters and at least 1 counting machine. Students Rights= State law requires both "domicile" and "a place of abode" to vote. The State Supreme Court has ruled that you must live in the election district with the intent to remain for an unlimited time. The Secretary of State's website includes a series of questions for student voters that includes misleading information and seems designed to discourage students. Student identification from public universities is accepted.*

Voter Education- *Sample Ballots= Sample ballots are not mailed to registered voters. Offline Distributes Virginia Easy Voter Guide booklets that explain right to see a sample ballot before voting and who to ask to see one. By Law Nothing in the Code can prohibit the creation of sample ballots. The electoral board may designate times and places for the exhibition of voting equipment containing sample ballots, for the purpose of informing voters who request instruction on the use of the equipment. Language Accessibility= Voting Rights Act, Sec. 203 Virginia's statewide population does not fall under Section 203. Secretary of State Website Information only available in English. Voting Machines= State Board of Elections Website List of voting equipment used by locality. Offline Distribute Virginia Easy Voter Guide booklets that include information on voters' rights for instructions on voting equipment. By Law "In each county, city, or town in which voting or counting equipment is to be used, the electoral board may designate times and places for the exhibition of equipment containing sample ballots, showing the title of offices to be filled, and, so far as practicable, the names of the candidates to be voted for at the next election for the purpose of informing voters who request instruction on the use of the equipment."*

Finally according to the Verified Voting Foundation Virginia is one of 11 States that not only have no voter verified paper record, they do not have any requirements for a voter verified paper record or voter audits. On their website is a "Verifier Map" of the United States if you click on the state of Virginia, you can find a breakdown by Counties and Cities. You will find that most counties and cities use Direct Recording Electronic machines. The AccuVote-TS DRE machine we use here in Virginia is a product of Diebold Election Systems. I can not prove that a "hacking of democracy" had taken or will take place here in Virginia, but then no one can prove otherwise.

Then there are the discrimination issues here in the State of Virginia, in particular here in the 7th Congressional District. Many people believe that it no longer exist here in Virginia. Reality proves different here in the home of the Confederacy Museum, especially when you factor in the election results mentioned above. There have been major changes as far as race is concern, but there are some things that are so obviously clear. As I traveled through the counties of the district I notice that there are more Confederate Flags flying full mast in many front lawns and have yet to see the State Flag or U.S. Flag displayed in that manner. I don't have a problem with the flag per se, it's what that flag represents. I don't have a problem with those who are proud of that heritage; at least I know where they stand. How do I run for public office and race not be a factor? While I am discussing this subject what about that of gender, again when we compare the election results to the issue, I can only conclude that the District is not ready to be represented by a woman. With having three daughters, that were raised to be very independent, I am concerned that my daughters get the same equal opportunity as your sons. This is just a few of the barriers I must destroy.

The other barrier is that during mid-term elections, not enough voters turn out to truly make a difference. Not to mention, enough voter interest that will make a difference either. With the turn out of this historic presidential election in 2008, just maybe people especially here in the State of Virginia, will pay attention and help me get a different type of election system instituted here. With what happened during the primaries in

Chesterfield County that alone should wake us up and start to pay attention. In 2000 the discrepancies in Florida won the election for George W. Bush, in 2004 the discrepancies in Ohio got him re-elected. With the turn out of this historic presidential election, just maybe we can show the new diversified Virginia by helping me destroy these barriers.

I plan to replicate that style of campaign that has worked so successfully by President Elect Barack Obama, "from the ground up." Now that you can appreciate the barriers that must be destroyed it brings me to why I must win?

Why I Must Win

Social, Economical and Political Change

The reason I must win is simple to effect progressive change. My stance on social issues is as follows:

- I believe that we the elected officials need to create a social environment in our respective districts, which people are not excluded from the activities of society, such as education, employment, or healthcare, on the basis of their sex, age, race, sexual orientation, religion, creed, national origin, physical or mental disability.

- I believe that marriage is sacred; something that is between a man and woman; and only religious institutions should perform those ceremonies. I further believe that these same religious institutions should make it more affordable and accessible for a man and woman to get married in their institutions. I furthermore believe that same sex civil unions should be carried out by each state and these unions should get the same respect as that of marriage. This in itself will keep the sanctity of the religious institutions and the sanctity of our constitution by keeping to the separation of church and state. Thereby not having the government creating laws forcing religious institutions do go against biblical doctrine.

- Personally I am pro-life, but until we as a people are ready to financially provide, and can guarantee that every unwanted child born, does not end up another statistic of abuse; misused; neglected, and permanently raised in a orphanage or similar institution; and is raised to be a productive member of society, then and only then should we do away with Roe vs. Wade. Since we as a people are unable to guarantee this I believe that all women should have access to birth control. I further support public funded contraception for poor women; the current ban on partial birth abortion; the education of reproduction and contraception, including abstinence and incentives for adoption.

- I believe that time restraints of general requirements of voters rights restoration should be reduced 100%. Instead of three year minimum waiting period after being released from supervised probation of a non-violent offense to apply for restoration, and instead of five year minimum waiting period after being released from supervised probation of a violent offense and or drug manufacturing or distribution offense to apply for restoration, it should be at the completion of the supervised probation with a recommendation by the Probation Officer. So many will miss the opportunity to participate in this historic presidential race, but I will do all I can to see that they will be able to participate in the historic re-election in 2012.

- I will support stem cell research under the strictest and ethical methods only. Instead of using donated stem cells of in vitro fertilization with the use of donated aborted stem cells, in that way an unwanted life is used to save an existing life. This will also ease the mental and emotional health of the woman whom chose to abort; in the knowledge that she is helping scientific research that may save a life.

My stance on economic issues is as follows:

- I will oppose tax cuts and other incentives going to oil companies. We need to give these tax breaks and other incentives to the American Auto Manufacturers in order to compete in the creation of the fuel efficient vehicles of tomorrow.

- I will support a progressive tax structure to provide more services and to reduce the injustice. I will support the reversing of tax cuts to the wealthiest American and the big corporations while putting in place tax cuts to the middle class and small businesses. I will oppose the cutting of social services, such as Social Security, Medicare and Medicaid.

- I will support a universal healthcare plan that would provide more people with affordable health insurance that covers essential services, achieve greater equity in access to care, realize efficiencies and cost savings in the provision of coverage and delivery of care, and redirect incentives to improve quality.

- I promise to fight to strengthen the laws that ensure that people will have clean air to breathe and clean water to drink. I further promise to ensure that these laws are enforced. I will protect hunting and fishing heritage by supporting conservation land expansions.

- Being a college student myself, I promise to fight to make a college education more affordable. I promise to further increase Pell Grants and college tuition tax deductions, until such time that a low-cost, publicly-funded college education is available to every eligible American student. I will fight to get more scholarships and other incentives for students and college institutions to discover safe, clean, reusable energy technology.

- Both NAFTA and CAFTA are dsesigned to push ahead the corporate globalization inititives that has caused the "race to the bottom" in labor and environmental standards and promotes privatization and deregulation of key public services. Since their implementation, we have watched the lost of over 3.5 million jobs, and record breaking product recalls annually. I will fight to reform these agreements.

My stance on foreign policy issues is as follows:

- I will support a redeployment of troops in Afghanistan to either captur or kill Osama Bin Laden and the other Al Quaeda leaders. My fears is that the mastermind of the September 11, 2001 attacks will die of natural causes before he is captured. This will leave the United States with the only option of having a posthumous execution, since he has already been found guilty in absentia.

- I personally stated my opposition to the Iraq War, because I could not understand how Saddam Hussein and his cronies was characterized as a eminent threat. Weapons of mass destruction was not only unfounded, but as described in the United Nation's speech by Gen. Collin Powell could not have reach the shores of the United States and the over dramatized vial of anthrax, neglected to say that the anthrax was no loner weapon grade. Not to mention that we had beaten the Iraqi Army into surrender, (including Saddam Hussein's elite guard) during Dessert Storm. But we must not leave without executing the right exit strategy that will give back the respect to our troops and our country deserve. The inclusion of the replacement of United States Troops with that of the United Nations Peace Keeping Forces.

- I am in support of unilateralism, which dictates that the United States should use military force without any assistance from other nations whenever it believes there exist a true eminent threat to its security or welfare. Meaning that the Sofaer's four elements must be established first.

My stance on legal issues is as follows:

- I am opposed to the use of torture against individuals apprehended and held prisoner; categorizing such prisoners as unlawful combatants by our military forces. By doing so does not release us from our obligations under the Geneva Conventions. Torture is inhumane; decreases our moral standing in the world and produces questionable results.
- I will fight to strengthen consumer protection rights especially against the unscrupulous harassing tactics of payday lending and rent to own businesses.
- Although I am a believer that "guns don't kill people…people kill people." I still would like to know the name of the sport or what animal is being hunted where a automatic weapon is needed? I am in strong support of H.R. 6257.

With the economy at an all time low; unemployment rate at a all time high; trillions of dollars in debt; a 750 billion dollar bailout of corporate America. Current politicians are still bickering whether or not to give a stimulus payments to her citizens. Because of

the experienced politicians in Washington D.C. we are in this mess. No wonder history

was made on November 4, 2008. we have a new leader of the free world; a new leader of

government change and the reason I believe no more excuses. President elect Barack

Obama has inspired me to take on this monumental task of running for U.S. Congress,

representing the 7th District of Virginia. He is the non-traditional leader we all need and I

am joining his army of non-traditional politicians. Non-traditional politicians moving into

the country's capital to restore the government to what the Founding Fathers intended to

be. A government of, for and by the people.

True Politician of the People, for the People, by the People

According to Frank Cornish a journalist from Daily Kos:

"Most Americans are not extreme on one side or the other. Most Americans want a government that will navigate controversial issues to come up with rational solutions that a majority of the electorate can support. Compromise, listening to all opinions, building consensus; these are the things that make for good government. Con. Eric Cantor does not compromise. He whines, he scapegoats, he manipulates; he is a free-market, corporate ideologue."

He further states in an October 14, 2008 article that:

"As you would expect the Abortion watch groups have him at 0 or 100 percent, that's not really beyond what we would expect on an issue like abortion; but look at all the other polarizing figures. Of particular interest checkout the section called "Conservative." Notice how old style conservative groups like the John Birch Society give him anywhere from 20-60%, while the newer pseudo-conservative groups give him 100% most of the time. He is nothing but a corporate tool. I guarantee that Barry Goldwater is spinning in his grave over these so called "conservatives." They are nothing more than corporate welfare recipients. They want only to privatize profits and socialize losses, and Eric Cantor is their little errand-boy."

This article was his endorsement of Anita Hartke the democratic challenger of Rep. Eric Cantor this year.

One thing that me and Mr. Cornish can agree on is that this year was the perfect time to take this seat from Rep. Cantor and turn the district blue. Where I differ from him is who should take the seat. I nor the citizens of this district believes that any democrat is better than being represented by Rep. Cantor. Now, the results of the Nov. 4, 2008 election proved one of two things. Either the results are that of election hacking or that we in this district will not vote along party lines just to replace Rep. Cantor and get a seat for the Democratic Party. That would make us democrats no better than the new conservatives. I truly wished I could have continued my race against Ms. Hartke in the Primary, because I am sure that I would have been the challenger, as well the overall winner of this election. But as I was reminded, "sometimes we can pick the time for opportunity…but oftentimes time picks you for the opportunity. In other words it was not my time. Ms. Hartke expected to be swept into office riding on the coattails: of her belated father's experience; Senator Elect Mark Warner and the Obama wave. Something she boldly stated in a interview. The people of this district are much smarter than most people give them credit for. They are not your traditional voter, they are a whole lot more politically aware today, and will not vote democratic straight down the line. Those are the voters I need to reach the new non-traditional voter. With this book, its promotion and sell is one of the ways I plan to use to raise critical seed money; get the message out; about me and what I am offering in alternative to Rep. Cantor.

This campaign is not against Ms. Anita Hartke, it is against Rep. Eric Cantor, so here is where I will draw the contrast between him and I. So instead of "Straight Talk" I will be "talking straight." I often time was amazed at some of Rep. Cantor's votes until I realized what his problems are. His major problem is that he is out of touch with his constituents. By supporting and voting on party lines caused this recession. And now the leadership of the Republican Party is desperately distancing themselves from the current administration as well as the responsibility of the state of our economy today. Rep. Cantor refusal to debate challengers further displays his unwillingness to compromise. It almost appears to be a complete arrogance to those that has put him into office. If not arrogance on his part, then it can only be he's taking his constituents for granted. Of the latter two I don't know which is worse, unless its both he's arrogantly taking his constituents for granted.

As I researched the final election results, I was taken aback to the documentary "Hacking Democracy." I was a bit confused at the Presidential, Senatorial and the Congressional results in the 7th Congressional District of Virginia in particular. There was only one county that was consistent in this district, this county is also the only county of the district that has DRE with Paper Ballot Verification. That county is Hanover, and it voted Republican across the board. What confused me is that the Senatorial race won more votes in the district than the Presidential and the Congressional. Now, one can conclude several things, election hacking, the district is not ready for a African American President, the district is not ready for a woman representative in Congress and or we have a new non-traditional voters in this district. Without paper ballot verifications any chance at proving voting hacking is impossible. I found it odd that Rep. Cantor voted no to HR 5803 and HR 5036, Backup Paper Ballot and Federal Funding for Voting System Changes respectively. All eyes were on the Presidential and Senate races, and none even paying the slightest attention to the Congressional race. I'll let you draw your own conclusions.

As I further researched Rep. Cantor and found him to be a classic example of the traditional politician. His latest campaign advertisement he boast of, "I have voted against Washington's wasteful spending of billions of taxpayers dollars." Now the key words in that statement is "wasteful spending." Let us take a look at Rep. Cantor's no record.

- HR 2638- Appropriates $22.88 billion for disaster relief and recovery, $480.25 billion for the Department of Defense, $43.48 billion for the Department of Homeland Security, and $119.92 billion for military construction and veterans affairs, maintains funding levels at $7.51 billion for 2009 to fund loans of up to $25 billion in total principal for automobile manufacturers and component suppliers to pay for up to 30% of the cost of equipping themselves to produce vehicles or components which meet specified emissions and fuel economy standards, appropriates $5.1 billion for low-income home energy assistance instead of the previous amount of $2.6 billion.
- HR 4137- Raises the maximum Pell grant from $5,800 to $8,000 per academic year by 2014, establishes federal grants to cover 50% of costs for colleges related to implementing emergency systems to notify the campus community of a significant emergency or dangerous situation through cellular, text message, or other advanced communication, and to develop procedures for the community to follow in case of an emergency or dangerous situation.
- HR 6331- Makes available an additional $100 million to aid states in giving assistance to low-income Medicare beneficiaries through September 30, 2008, and makes available a total of $600 million through December 31, 2009, removes life insurance policy values from being factored into determining an individual's income eligibility for Medicare low-income subsidies, allocates $7.5 million in federal funding for State Health Insurance Assistance Programs based on the number of eligible individuals and the number of rural beneficiaries to be used for Medicare and Medicaid services and to implement outreach programs to enroll eligible low-income individuals, authorizes $210 million for the Secretary of Health and Human Services to give grants to states to increase mental health and other health services to veterans of Operation Iraqi Freedom and Operation Enduring Freedom living in rural areas.
- HR 2642- Designates differing amounts of payments to be made to fund the higher education of individuals who have served on active duty in the Armed Forces beginning on or after September 11, 2001 based on factors such as length of active duty service and disabilities accrued, and specifies

that these payments shall not exceed the cost of in-state tuition at the most expensive public university in the state in which the individual is enrolled, requires the Secretary of Defense to match assistance given to members of the Armed Forces by institutions of higher learning to cover fees and expenses beyond what other provisions of this amendment provide.

- HR 3043- $13.63 billion for the Department of Labor, including $3.37 billion for training and employment services, $3.47 billion for state unemployment insurance and employment service operations, and $1.65 billion for the office of the Job Corps, $480.03 billion for the Department of Health and Human Services, including $30.01 billion for the National Institutes of Health, $401.41 billion for the Centers for Medicare and Medicaid Services, and $27.32 billion for the Administration for Children and Families, 63.58 billion for the Department of Education, including $16.38 billion for student financial assistance, $15.93 billion for education for the disadvantaged, and $12.36 billion for special education, $53.98 for related agencies, including $51.81 billion for the Social Security Administration, $1.35 billion for the Corporation for National and Community Service, and $420 million for the Corporation for Public Broadcasting.
- HR 976- Appropriates $9.13 billion for fiscal year 2008, $10.68 billion for fiscal year 2009, $11.85 billion for fiscal year 2010, and $13.75 billion for fiscal year 2011 for CHIP, appropriates $100 million for grants to eligible private or public entities to conduct outreach efforts designed to increase CHIP enrollment among eligible children and sets aside 10% of the allocated money for the administration of a national CHIP enrollment campaign.
- HR 1- To provide for the implementation of the recommendations of the National Commission on Terrorist Attacks upon the United States.
- HR 3061- $49.3 billion for discretionary education funding, $23 billion for National Institute of Health, $14.1 billion for the Department of Labor, $6.5 billion for Head Start program, $4.1 billion for Centers for Disease Control, with $339 million in funding directed towards bioterrorism preparedness.

After checking through a list, (77 pages) of major bills and the votes of Rep. Cantor, I had a problem finding the "wasteful spending" in those previous bills. Maybe you can, I did find some very interesting votes that Rep. Cantor voted yes too. Rep. Cantor voted along party lines with concern to the National budget spending and helped to get us into this huge debt and current recession issue. Since I am talking straight, it would be inexcusable of me not to list them:

- HR 1424- Vote to concur with Senate amendments and pass a bill that allows the Secretary of the Treasury to purchase troubled assets from financial institutions, with a total outstanding balance of up to $700 billion, and provides tax incentives for alternative energies and contains income tax and alternative minimum tax provisions. (Note: this is the second version, the first version did not include the economic package and he also voted yes on it).
- HR 5715-Increases the loan limit above the determined financial need for graduate students enrolled in an eligible institution from $10,000 to $12,000, allows a limit of up to $2,000 for dependent undergraduate students, and increases the limit amounts for independent undergraduate students from $4,000 to $6,000 for the first two years of study and from $5,000 to $7,000 for the second two years of study.
Increases the total federal loan limit for undergraduate studies from $23,000 to $31,000 for dependent students and from $46,000 to $57,500 for independent students.
Allows a six-month grace period after a student has less than half of a full time class load before parent borrowers must start making payments.
Authorizes the Secretary of Education and the Secretary of the Treasury to purchase loans originated on or after October 1, 2003 from eligible lenders if there is an inadequate availability of loan capital to meet the demand for student loans, with a temporary authority that expires on July 1, 2009.
- HR 5631-$119.05 billion for operation and maintenance of the Department of Defense, $86.35 billion for military personnel, including $25.91 billion for the Army, $20.29 billion for the Air Force, $19.05 million for the Navy, and $7.93 billion for the Marine Corps.
$80.59 billion for the procurement of aircraft, weapons and ammunition for the Army, Navy, Marine Corps and Air Force.
$70 billion for ongoing operations in Iraq and Afghanistan.
$75.44 million for research, development, test and evaluation.
- HR 5672-$22.73 billion for scientific programs, including $16.71 billion for NASA and $6.01 billion for the National Science Foundation.
$22.23 billion for the Department of Justice, including $5.96 billion for the FBI.
$10.78 billion for other agencies, including $7.5 billion for the Business Loans Programs Account.
$7.67 billion for the Department of Commerce.
$7.36 billion for the Department of State, including $2.26 billion for International Organizations and Peace Keeping.
- HR 4939- $70.58 billion for "Global War on Terrorism," including: (Title I)
$65.91 billion for the Department of Defense, including: (Title I, Chapter 2).
$37.9 billion for operation and maintenance.
$15.03 billion for procurement of aircraft, missiles, weapons, combat vehicles, and ammunition.

$10.28 billion for military personnel.
$1.69 billion for Economic Support Fund (I,3).
$1.38 billion for diplomatic and consular affairs of the Administration of Foreign Affairs (I,6).
- HR 4613- $25 billion for emergency defense spending for operations in Iraq and Afghanistan.
$104.2 billion for military personnel.
$120.6 billion for military operations and equipement maintenance.
$77.4 billion for the procurement of new weapons.
-

Now, I could have listed more, but I did not want to be publishing Rep. Eric I. Cantor's voting record. Let us not forget the rubber stamping of the funding for the Iraq War. As I delved deeper into these votes, I was able to find statements made by Rep. Cantor at the time of each vote and found some very strange statements. It appears that Rep. Cantor is not just positioning for a better leadership post, but maybe considering a run for President soon. If he can prove to Republican colleagues he can handle the tough questions. From the transcripts of statements he has made and videos of interviews he has done, he needs some more work. But then, he does have an additional four years to get it together. I wonder should I be looking forward to him debating me in 2010, since he has successfully been reelected without being in even one. I must say, I truly didn't expect to see him in interviews with media that is more liberal than they are conservative. I know that he loves doing interviews with those who favor conservatism and Rep. Cantor. Fox and local Fox affiliates are the media that will never ask Rep. Cantor the tough questions.

Rep. Cantor introduced a bill back in January 16, 2008 HR 4995, and I am still trying to figure out is this: Country First; Corporations First, Citizens First? I am also trying to figure out why is it so hard to find information other than his introduction of bill statement at a press conference? Here is the bill itself: Middle Class Jobs Protection Act of 2008 - Amends the Internal Revenue Code to: (1) reduce the maximum corporate income tax rate to 25%; (2) increase the expensing allowance for depreciable business assets to $250,000 in 2008 and 2009; (3) increase to 50% the current year bonus depreciation allowance for certain property placed in service in 2008 and 2009; and (4) allow additional carry backs for certain net operating losses and for excess business and foreign tax credit amounts arising in 2008 and 2009. I just have one question, where is the protection of middle class jobs? I see nothing except the protection of corporate profits, or the assurance of corporate profits. Because of this trickle down economic theory we are in this mess we are currently in. Not to mention, Rep. Cantor wants to make sure that corporate executives continue to get there "golden parachute," even though it's a limited amount.

Rep. Cantor thinks that if he calls it something other than what it really is, we the people will not notice it and vote him back into office. Rep. Cantor can't even take personal responsibility for the state of our economy. Yes, pointing the finger is not going to fix the problem. But in order to restore the public confidence in our government, in our economy and be willing to sacrifice to get it right, someone has to take responsibility, or be held accountable.

I mentioned all this to simply say, that Rep. Cantor can not be allowed to continue this obsession with Big Corporations and their Executives. I truly believe that the demographics here in the 7th Congressional District of Virginia have changed. We can not let Rep. Cantor continue his arrogance and taken the citizens of this district for granted. It's time we hold him accountable. Make him explain why we should keep him as the Representative of this district in 2010.

True Change of Progression

Again, I truly believe that the demographics here in the 7th Congressional District of Virginia have changed. I do perceive that some traditional voters fighting and resisting that change. I however, deeply believe that more new non-traditional voters than traditional voters, which will help the district display its diversity. One thing has been proven from the results of the Congressional race is that more often voters have had enough of the partisan politics as usual and by 2010 there will be even more.

As a Blue Dog Democrat, I am offering to the citizens of the 7th Congressional District of Virginia true fiscal conservatism. We don't have a tax problem in this country, we have a spending problem. As a person whom has learned the hard way what consequences come when you over spend money. We are borrowing money from countries that should not be trusted, to pay countries we do not trust. Current government officials are spending money as though a money tree grows somewhere in D.C. we need to get to a balanced budget and start paying down on this huge deficit created by a supposedly fiscal conservative controlled House for six years. We have watched over again where "middle class protection" talking points turned out to be no more than corporate welfare. Allowing golden parachutes for executives whom helped run our economy into the ground.

I intend to take true fiscal conservatism to the U.S. House of Representatives. Help President Elect Barack Obama keep his promise of "Change" to government and be one of the leaders making sure that it progresses accordingly. I don't agree with him totally on certain issues, but I do see him as a President that will be more Centrist than any other President to date. I will certainly be working as a bi-partisan government official for true progressive change of the people, for the people and by the people of the 7th Congressional District of Virginia.

The President Elect Obama has promised to reverse the Bush Administration's tax cuts, to finally work for the middle class people of the country for a change. I do support this position for the reason that the more money the consumer has the more money will be spent to increase sales of all corporations across the board. To believe that the tax cuts given to corporations will increase profits and the labor force is naïve thinking at best, especially since we have seen record unemployment rates throughout this administration's tenure. I will fight to get those tax breaks for corporations that took there business overseas and left here at home unemployed middle class citizens: taken from them, give the tax breaks to those patriotic corporations that stayed here, and tried to help the average citizen keep a job and keep our economy sound. The Wall Street Bailout was something I truly would have not supported unless there was more oversight and guaranteed deal similar to that of Warren Buffet's. The taxpayers of the United States should have been represented as investors and not as philanthropists.

I also believe that the invasion of Iraq was wrong and I further believe that we can not just cut and run. Our withdrawal of troops must be done in a way that the United States will retain and or regain its respect around the world. I propose that we replace United States Military Force with United Nations Peace Keeping Forces. With a presence no longer than what is necessary for the new government of Iraq to be able to stand alone.

The other thing that is most important to me is Campaign and Election Reformation, and first on that agenda would be the way we elect our officials. We should have a voting system that includes paper ballot verifications, to restore confidence in the system. I would also be looking to get certain former convicted felons their rights to vote back, restored to them upon the completion of all timed served, as they will be able to help out in the historical reelection of President Barack Obama. I further support term limits of the U.S. House of Representatives and Senate, six two year term for Congress and two six year term for the Senate. This would allow for younger blood, newer ideas, fresher thoughts provided by more non-traditional politicians. Take a long look in the mirror and behold a Portrait of a Non-Traditional Politician

Conclusion

Now that the historical election in United States History is finally over and many of us our totally emotionally and physically drained, we only have two months before the inauguration. I am sure everyone is resting up for the hard work ahead. We are entrenched in two wars; our economy is in the worst condition ever. We are literally one bad decision from a depression far worst than the one before. Not to mention all the other campaign promises. Now the Big Three Automakers are in trouble. Debate of let them go, I refused to let a cornerstone of American Democracy be replaced by foreign entities. We need to help them out with oversight that they will build better fuel efficient vehicles in order to compete against foreign automakers.

Here is how you can help me, help you. Tell your friends and family members about this book, urged them to buy it, proceeds of this book will be going to my campaign. I am going to need Senior Campaign Manager, County Campaign Mangers across the district. If you are interested and eager to help me win in 2010 and live in one of these Counties: Caroline, Chesterfield, Culpeper, Goochland, Hanover, Henrico, Louisa, Madison, Orange, Page, Rappahannock, Spotsylvania or the Northern Section of

Richmond City then you can send me a copy of your resume via e-mail to btent714@yahoo.com. These positions will of course, be paid positions that will be discussed at a later time. If you live in any of the aforementioned counties and are willing to host a book signing event in your home then send your contact information via e-mail to btent714@yahoo.com.

You can also help by going to my website and show your financial support at www.briantaylor4congress.com. You can meet me from time to time at your local County Democratic Committee Meeting. I will be also doing Book signing events at your local Bookstore, check my websites for dates and time. Thank you and always remember "Yes We Can!" Now Let's "get fired up and ready to go!"

References

American Heritage Dictionary: Fourth Edition, Boston: Houghton Mifflin, 2000

Brennan Center for Research: www.brennancenter.org

CNN: Black In America, Soledad O'Brien, 2008

Common Cause: www.commoncause.org

Dictionary.com: dictionary.reference.com

Merriam Webster Dictionary: www.merriam-webster.com

Pew Research Center: www.people-press.org

United States Census Bureau: www.census.gov

Verified Voting Foundation: www.verifedvoting.org

Webster II New College Dictionary: Houghton Mifflin, 1995

Wikipedia: www.wikipedia.org

http://en.wikipedia.org/wiki/Republican_Party_(United_States)_presidential_primaries,_
2008

http://en.wikipedia.org/wiki/Democratic_Party_(United_States)_presidential_primaries,_
2008

http://en.wikipedia.org/wiki/United_States_presidential_election,_2008

http://www.warsearch.com/topic/Republican_Party_(United_States)

http://en.wikipedia.org/wiki/Democratic_Party_(United_States)_presidential_primaries,_
2008

Hacking Democracy: by Simon Ardizzone, Russell Michaels and Robert Carrillo Cohen
The documentary exposes the dangers of voting machines used during America's mid
term and presidential elections. Electronic voting machines count approximately 90% of
America's votes in county, state and federal elections. Filmed over three years this expos'
follows the investigations of a team of citizen activists and hackers as they take on the
electronic voting industry, targeting the Diebold corporation. "Hacking Democracy"
uncovers incendiary evidence from the trash cans of Texas to the ballot boxes of Ohio,
exposing secrecy, votes in the trash, hackable software and election officials rigging the
presidential recount. Ultimately proving our votes can be stolen without a trace "Hacking
Democracy" culminates in the famous 'Hursti Hack'; a duel between the Diebold voting
machines and a computer hacker from Finland - with America's democracy at stake.

www.hackingdemocracy.com

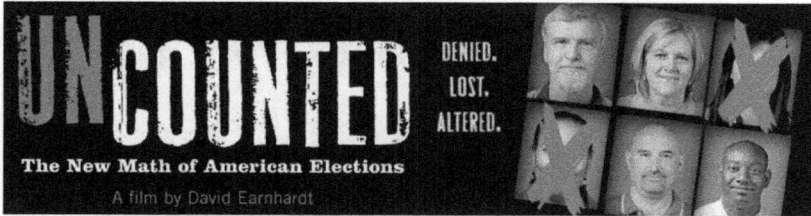

Uncounted: Was the 2004 U.S. Presidential Election on the Level? This revealing documentary shows how suppression tactics, voting machine security breaches, and vote count manipulation threaten our democracy.

www.uncountedthemovie.com

Iraq for Sale: No conflict has been as money making for corporations as the Iraq War. Follow the story as "private contractors" are present at Abu Ghraib, Falloujah and other hotspots, turning mayhem into profits.

www.iraqforsale.org